UNITED STATES EMPLOYMENT AND TRAINING PROGRAMS

UNITED STATES EMPLOYMENT AND TRAINING PROGRAMS

A Selected Annotated Bibliography

Compiled by Frederick A. Raffa, Clyde A. Haulman, and Djehane A. Hosni

Greenwood Press
Westport, Connecticut • London, England

Library of Congress Cataloging in Publication Data

Raffa, Frederick A.
    United States employment and training programs.

    Includes indexes.
    1. Manpower policy—United States—Bibliography.
I. Haulman, Clyde A.   II. Hosni, Djehane A.   III. Title.
Z7164.L1R33   1983   [HD5724]   016.3311'0973   82-25108
ISBN 0-313-23872-3 (lib. bdg.)

Library of Congress Catalog Card Number: 82-25108
ISBN: 0-313-23872-3

First published in 1983

Greenwood Press
A division of Congressional Information Service, Inc.
88 Post Road West, Westport, Connecticut 06881

Printed in the United States of America

10 9 8 7 6 5 4 3 2 1

Contents

Acknowledgments

The authors wish to express their appreciation for the support and encouragement of colleagues, friends, and family. In particular, the authors are indebted to the U.C.F. College of Business Administration and to the Florida State Department of Labor and Employment Security under whose auspices the initial research was undertaken.

The authors also extend their sincere appreciation for the time and technical expertise provided by Judy Ryder, Lynn Schuster, Teresa Sullivan, Tamera Comish, Edward M. Foster, and Jonathan Guyton, as well as for the coordination and organizational efforts of Michael McLane.

Introduction

The dramatic growth in United States employment and training programs over the past decade has resulted in significant interest in program planning, development, and mechanisms for delivery. Not unexpectedly, a considerable volume of research and publication has emerged. To date, however, manpower and employment researchers have had only limited bibliographic materials available to assist in defining and delineating the subject area. Much of this bibliographic work, including limited abstracts of principal research, has been found in the American Economic Association's Journal of Economic Literature, under Section 800--Manpower, Labor and Population. Additional bibliographic material had been available in the U.S. Department of Labor's now discontinued publications entitled Publications of the Bureau of Labor Statistics. Of limited assistance from the U.S. Department of Labor is the inventory of research and evaluation projects funded by the Office of the Assistant Secretary for Policy, Evaluation and Research (ASPER). The ASPER summaries involve work completed during the 1970-1979 period and are limited primarily to work done under contract with ASPER.

The following collection of abstracts was developed as a specific aide to those individuals who desire a complete and precise review of research in the increasingly important field of U.S. Employment and Training Programs.

A. Background on U. S. Employment and Training Programs

The passage of the Comprehensive Employment and Training Act (CETA) on December 28, 1973, introduced a new manpower system designed to "provide job training and employment opportunities for the economically disadvantaged, unemployed, and underemployed."[1] The legislation creating CETA had evolved out of the manpower programs of the sixties. Continued high unemployment and poverty in the midst of an otherwise prosperous economy led in 1962 to the passage of the Manpower Development and Training Act (MDTA). The MDTA legislation had come in response to a report from a special Senate committee on unemployment that had alerted and alarmed senators with the scenario of adult male family heads without jobs as a result of automation. Not unexpectedly, the MDTA legislation was principally aimed at retraining the technologically unemployed. However, by the time the program finally got underway, unemployment had decreased and those left out of work were principally new entrants into the labor force. Consequently, the new MDTA participants were primarily those labor force members who had little in the way of any formal education, training, or experience. In partial response to this new-entrant enrollment, Congress in 1963 passed the Vocational Education Act providing significant increases in the funding of vocational education on a revised assumption that nearly everyone needed specific occupational preparation.

During this same time, the Civil Rights movement had begun to gather support from a broader spectrum of population and culminated in the passage of the Economic Opportunity Act (EOA) in 1964. This new legislation was, in the words of President Lyndon B. Johnson, to be a total war on poverty. The principal focus of the EOA was the breaking of the cycle of poverty by providing education, training, and job preparation to those who had traditionally suffered most from unemployment. A central focus of the EOA was on disadvantaged youth and community action programs. Consistent with this focus, EOA funding was responsible for the creation of the Neighborhood Youth Corps (NYC)--a job creation program for poor high school students and dropouts; the Job Corps--a residential training and basic education program for school dropouts handicapped by their family environment; and the Work Experience and Training program which required local community coordination of programs for welfare recipients. The MDTA program that had initially operated as a program of aid to all of the nation's unemployed was gradually transformed into a weapon of the war on poverty, with its principal focus on the economically disadvantaged. Amendments to the Economic Opportunity Act in 1966 and 1967 added small-scale job creation to the program arsenal and resulted in the creation of the Concentrated Employment Program (CEP). The objectives of the CEP were twofold: (1) to concentrate the efforts of federal manpower programs in those areas hardest hit by high unemployment and low income conditions; and (2) to recruit private employers to hire the economically disadvantaged. Although this second objective was a rather significant failure, it did set the stage for the 1968 announcement by President Lyndon Johnson of the creation of the National Alliance of Businessmen to administer a Job Opportunities in the Business Sector program (NAB-JOBS). The success of the NAB-JOBS program was beyond expectation. Although the program provided subsidies to private employers who hired the economically disadvantaged, only one-third of the employer participants ever accepted any compensation. Unfortunately, the overall assessment of the NAB-JOBS program is somewhat clouded. Some attributed the success of the program to the widespread labor shortage. Since those firms who accepted no compensation were not obligated to file reports or submit to audits, it was difficult to determine exactly what changes had taken place that would not have otherwise emerged out of the labor shortage situation. A change in administrations diminished the personal involvement of the executive office, while Congress moved to approve new programs to deal with the emerging manpower problems. A fragmented manpower system evolved that included, in addition to the elements already presented such programs as the Work Incentive program (WIN)--a program designed to provide funding for public assistance recipients to achieve economic independence; and the Emergency Employment Act of 1971 (EEA)--issued in response to the unemployment resulting from the 1971 recession. Confusion, duplication and considerable overlap resulted from this proliferation of programs. Each one had its own structure, clientele, and delivery mechanism. Not unexpectedly, there was growing sentiment in the federal government to consider some type of reform of the manpower system.

The emerging manpower philosophy of the 1970s increasingly embraced program decentralization and decategorization. This philosophy sought to reduce the restrictive federal regulations on the use of employment and training program funds by state and local governments, thus broadening the range of program activities as well as the groups to be served while permitting greater flexibility in the administrative systems for program delivery. This "new federalism" advocated employment and training programs more responsive to individual and local needs, that is, programs that recognized the uniqueness of local employment and training problems.[2]

When the Comprehensive Employment & Training Act (CETA) was passed by Congress in December 1973, its twin goals encompassed the decentralization and decategorization of United States manpower programs. A major feature of the bill provided authority for counties as well as cities and states to become prime sponsors, with preference given to the smallest governmental units. The prime sponsor could choose which clients to serve, what services to offer them, and which organizations to employ for the delivery of services.

Since its inception, CETA has been subjected to economic conditions that no United States manpower program has encountered since the 1930s. In the late 1960s inflation had persisted at high levels as a result of the expansionary effects of the Vietnam War spending and the reluctance of Congress to offset this stimulus with tax increases. As a result, the nation began to experience a rollercoaster ride of high rates of inflation followed by bouts of high unemployment as successive administrations and congresses vacillated between the two issues. Finally, beginning in 1972, a series of events that included poor world agricultural yields, the devaluation of the United States dollar and exchange rate upheaval, as well as the fourfold increase in oil prices by OPEC, combined to produce the highest United States unemployment rates since 1940 and, in a new twist, persistently high inflation rates.

Congress was under severe pressure to deal with these problems and concentrated on reducing unemployment. This was contrary to the wishes of the Ford administration, which saw inflation as the greater threat. Congress's actions took two forms. First, a new title was added to CETA that provided $2.5 billion to create 300,000 state and local government jobs. Congress coupled this with a temporary extension and expansion of unemployment insurance benefits. Still the high unemployment lingered on, peaking at 9 percent in 1975. Indeed, the subsequent 7.7 percent unemployment rate during 1976 has been said to have contributed to Gerald Ford's defeat in the presidential elections.

Following up on campaign pledges to reduce unemployment, Congress and the Carter administration increased the CETA budget from $7 billion to $11 billion and expanded the number of PSE positions from 300,000 to 725,000. This action was followed in 1977 by the implementation of the Youth Employment and Demonstration Projects Act (YEDPA) which budgeted $1 billion (partly allocated to CETA) to provide jobs and training for unemployed youths.

In 1978, CETA came up for Congressional reauthorization. Congress faced significant pressure to retreat from the ideals of decentralization and decategorization that had produced CETA initially. The news media were full of stories concerning misappropriation of funds including the use of CETA funds for regular city and county positions, nepotism and favoritism in the allocation of PSE slots, and outright theft of funds. Moreover, some members of Congress were less than satisfied with a process that called for them to appropriate CETA funds but allowed city and county officials to take credit for dispensing them to their constituents. Not unexpectedly, city and county officials were very pleased with the status quo and successfully lobbied for a CETA reauthorization bill that only slightly blunted the broad local discretion granted in the original bill of 1973. The major changes written into the reauthorization bill included:

- All CETA services including PSE were limited to the economically disadvantaged and long-term unemployed.
- The maximum allowable for salaries for PSE workers was lowered considerably.
- Limits were placed on the enrollment duration of individuals in PSE and work experience programs.
- Five billion dollars was appropriated to create the new Title VII which directed interested prime sponsors to create private industry councils (PICs) in cooperation with the private sector to provide private employment for the economically disadvantaged.[3]

President Ronald Reagan was elected on a platform of reduced government spending, and to date his administration has not been favorably inclined toward CETA. As high unemployment rates are still being experienced in an inflationary economy, CETA is being closely scrutinized. In fiscal year 1980, CETA-allocated expenditures totaled $9.6 billion. The new administration has cut the CETA budget to $3.5 billion in 1981 with additional cuts to be made in 1982. The cuts were aimed at the Public Service Employment (PSE) program and call for its phasing out by the end of fiscal year 1981 (despite the fact that during the past five years, approximately one-half of all CETA expenditures have been designed to create PSE jobs). The administration feels that although there is an important role for government in the employment picture, it is the private sector that provides most of the jobs in the American economy. Indeed, five out of every six new jobs are created in the private sector. Since the ultimate success of the CETA manpower program depends on the transition of participants into unsubsidized employment, the Reagan administration is not unexpectedly supportive of a more effective level of private sector involvement in the nation's manpower programs.

Thus, under the Reagan administration the CETA program faces a considerable overhaul. This new round of changes will involve considerable evaluation of the CETA program as the Reagan administration seeks to reshape it into a viable manpower program, justifying the still significant government investment.

B.   Scope of the Bibliography

The bibliography is designed to encompass the most important works relating to employment and training programs in the period 1970 to the present. The major focus of the work is on the Comprehensive Employment and Training Act (CETA), the current institutional framework for the delivery of many elements of United States employment and training programs. However, because CETA is not the only delivery system currently providing training and because CETA grew out of the varied experiences of the 1960s and early 1970s, in particular the Manpower Development and Training Act and the Emergency Employment Act, works dealing with both pre-CETA programs and other programs are included.

Publications included in the bibliography consist of books, professional journal articles, reports by private research organizations and reports and other publications by United States government agencies. Most are from the 1970s and early 1980s, although occasionally a work from the late 1960s has been included.

C.   Methodology for Identifying and Selecting Entries

Potential entries for the bibliography were obtained from a number of sources. The DIALOG computer information service was used with entries obtained from CIS (Congressional Information Service, Inc.), ERIC (Educational Resources Information Center), Social SciSearch (Institute for Scientific Information), Economics Abstracts International (Learned Information Ltd.), and the GPO (Government Printing Office) Monthly Catalog. In addition, the Monthly Catalog of United States Government Publications, the American Economic Association's quarterly Journal of Economic Literature, and the U.S. Department of Labor's Monthly Labor Review were used to identify possible bibliography entries.

Having identified potential entries, each was located and evaluated by one of the authors. In general, the authors attempted to select work that would be considered as a principal contribution in the field. Anticipating that the bibliography might well serve as a framework for future research, the team was especially conscious of methodological contributions and the application or testing of pertinent hypotheses in the field of employment and training. Where possible, application studies which held broad policy making implications were included, while those that involved the duplication of an existing study or a limited geographic area were excluded. As a consequence, the bibliography possesses not only the character of a methodological inquiry and review, but simultaneously serves as an effective survey of the principal attempts at testing and validating pertinent employment and training hypotheses.

D.   Entries and Annotations

Each entry in the bibliography lists author or authors, title, publisher, place and date of publication, as well as the Superintendent of Documents or National Technical Information Service (NTIS) number, as appropriate. In the case of journal articles, the name and date of the journal, volume, and pages are also included. The annotations come from a number of sources. The majority are annotations by one of the three authors of the bibliography. Those annotations that were taken from another source were done so with the permission of the original source indicated by an abbreviation at the end of the annotation. The abbreviations for the sources of these annotations are:

CIS   Reprinted by permission of the Congressional Information Service.

ILRR   Reprinted by permission of the Industrial and Labor Relations Review, Cornell University. All rights reserved.

JEL   Reprinted by permission of the Journal of Economic Literature.

JHR

Reprinted by permission of the <u>Journal of Human Resources</u>, University of Wisconsin Press, Board of Regents, University of Wisconsin System.

NTIS

References from the NTIS Bibliographic Data Base reprinted by permission from the National Technical Information Service, U.S. Department of Commerce.

UAQ

Reprinted by permission of the <u>Urban Affairs Quarterly</u>.

E.   Arrangement of the Bibliography

The bibliography entries are arranged in alphabetical order by author. The Subject Index includes the most important topic areas in the field and refers the user to the bibliography entry number and title. Because some subject areas have such a large number of entries, the titles are included as a means of further identifying the literature.

To further assist the user of this bibliography, a list of Abbreviations, a Directory of Publishers, and an Author Index are also included.

F.   <u>Notes</u>

1.   Public Law 93-203, The Comprehensive Employment and Training Act (CETA), 93rd Congress, S.1559, December 28, 1973.

2.   Sar A. Levitan and Joyce K. Zickler, <u>Quest for a Federal Manpower Partnership</u> (Cambridge, Mass.:   Harvard University Press, 1974), p. 34.

3.   Sar A Levitan, Garth L. Mangum, and Ray Marshall, <u>Human Resources and Labor Markets</u> (New York: Harper & Row, 1981), pp. 320-23.

Abbreviations

AFDC	Aid to Families with Dependent Children
ARA	Area Redevelopment Act of 1961
ASPER	Assistant Secretary for Policy, Evaluation and Research U.S. Department of Labor
AZEUD	Arizona Employment and Unemployment Data Set
CBO	Community-Based Organizations
CDC	Community Development Corporations
CETA	Comprehensive Employment and Training Act
CETA-PSE	Comprehensive Employment and Training Act-Public Service Employment
CEETP	Committee on Evaluation of Employment and Training Program, National Academy of Science
CLMS	Continuous Longitudinal Manpower Survey
CPS	Current Population Survey
CT	Classroom Training
CWBH	Continuous Wage and Benefit History
CWHS	Continuous Work History Sample, Social Security Administration
DAJ	Dual Aspect Jobs
DJC	Direct Job Creation
DOL	Department of Labor
EATS	Monmouth County Welfare Board Employments and Training Unit
EDA	Economic Development Administration
EEA	Emergency Employment Act
EJEAA	Emergency Jobs and Employment Assistance Act
EJPEA	Emergency Job Program Extension Act of 1976
EOA	Economic Opportunity Act
ES	Earnings Subsidy
ETA	Employment and Training Administration, U.S. Dept. of Labor
EVSI	Expected Value of Sample Information
GAO	General Accounting Office
GPO	Government Printing Office
JC	Job Corps
JOBS	Job Opportunities in the Business Sector
LEED	Longitudinal Employee-Employer Data
MARS	Manpower Automated Reporting System
MDC	Manpower Development Corporation
MDTA	Manpower Development and Training Act
NAIRU	Nonaccelerating Inflation Rate of Unemployment
NCEP	National Commission for Employment Policy (formerly National Commission for Manpower Policy)
NCMP	National Commission for Manpower Policy (now National Commission for Employment Policy)

NIT	Negative Income Tax
NJES	New Jersey Employment Service
NJTC	New Jobs Tax Credit section of the Tax Reduction and Simplification Act of 1977
NPSPS	National Program for Selected Population Segments
NYC	Neighborhood Youth Corps
NYC/OS	Neighborhood Youth Corps/Out of School Component
OEDP	Overall Economic Development Program
OIC	Opportunities Industrialization Centers
OJT	On-the-Job Training
PBJI	Program for Better Jobs and Income
PEP	Public Employment Program
PIC	Private Industry Council
PSE	Public Service Employment
PWIP	Public Works Impact Program
SEPS	Subsidized Employment in the Public Sector
SPEDY	Summer Program for Economically Disadvantaged Youth
STIP	Skill Training Improvement Program
SWP	Special Work Project
TIPP	Training Incentives Payments Program
UI	Unemployment Insurance
WE	Work Experience
WIN	Work Incentive Program
WRS	Wage Rate Subsidy
YEDPA	Youth Employment and Demonstration Projects

UNITED STATES EMPLOYMENT AND TRAINING PROGRAMS

Bibliography

1. Abt Associates, Inc. Evaluation of the Skill Training Improvement
Program (STIP): Phase I (Follow-up). Washington, D.C.: Employment and
Training Administration, 1979. L37.2:SK3

This evaluation of the Skill Training Improvement Program (STIP)
focuses on the success of CETA prime sponsors in starting and
implementing advanced skill training projects and on the role of
the private sector in the program. It has two objectives. One is
to determine the types of projects set up with STIP funds and to
relate these project types to significant local strategies and
factors which account for major variations and patterns among them.
The second is to determine the factors which significantly affect
operational performance and to assess the strengths and weaknesses
of various designs during their implementation phase, paying
special attention to changes in design and emphasis. Volume One
presents a summary of preliminary findings, a cross-site review of
project characteristics, and an analysis of specific program
aspects. Volume Two presents one-page project summaries of all 141
STIP projects.

2. Abt Associates, Inc. New Approaches to CETA Training: An Overview
of the Title III National Program for Selected Population Segments.
Washington, D.C.: Employment and Training Administration, 1979.
L37.14:69

The National Program for Selected Population Segments (NPSPS), a
group of 82 projects aimed at special population segments such as
women, youth, handicapped workers, rural workers, ex-offenders and
older workers is reviewed in this report. The projects were funded
during fiscal year 1977 and were designed to provide participants
with benefits not available under general CETA Title I programs,
test innovative models, and serve groups which had not previously
received specialized employment and training services. The three
objectives were met by NPSPS as a whole with 44 percent of the
responding projects being refunded. While not a radical departure
in employment and training programs, NPSPS made incremental changes
which benefited the targeted special groups.

3. Abt Associates, Inc. The Noneconomic Impacts of the Job Corps.
Washington, D.C.: Employment and Training Administration, 1978.
L37.14: 64

The purpose of this study was to develop measures of the noneconomic benefits of the Job Corps and apply them to a limited sample of Job Corps participants and a comparison group. The measures developed and used fall into three categories: job related impacts, social-attitudinal impacts and health and educational impacts. For the twenty-one specific outcomes considered, those participants who remained in the Job Corps at least three months improved on eight different outcomes, compared to two for those who dropped out and five for those who did not enroll. The Job Corps improvements occurred in all three areas of noneconomic benefits. Other findings suggest that the Job Corps should re-examine its post-program placement system, that operations differ greatly among Job Corps centers with some centers being more worthy of replication than others, and that the Job Corps must make an effort to either screen out those who seem unlikely to survive the first weeks or to strengthen the program so that more enrollees will remain long enough to benefit.

4.   Abt Associates, Inc. Overcoming Discriminating Barriers to Public Employment. Cambridge, Massachusetts: Abt Associates, Inc., 1974. PB-237 376/9GI

The report presents guidance on how to diagnose barriers to equal employment opportunity in state and local governments and ways to help overcome such barriers. It is based largely on an evaluation of a program, PACE MAKER, which worked in 1970-72 with eight state and local governments to revise employment practices which discriminated against the disadvantaged. (NTIS)

5.   Ashenfelter, Orley. Estimating the Effect of Training Programs on Earnings with Longitudinal Data. Washington, D.C.: U.S. Department of Labor, 1976. NTIS PB281193/AS

This study is concerned with the effect of training programs on earnings and the difficulty of implementing an adequate experimental design to obtain a group against which to compare trainees' reliably. The researcher matched the program record of each trainee with the trainee's social security earnings history, concentrating on those entering classroom training under the Manpower Development and Training Act (MDTA) in the first 3 months of 1964. Results indicate that: (1) All of the trainee groups suffered unpredicted earnings declines in the year prior to training. The estimates of these declines ranged from $150 to $350, being in the lower range for black trainees and in the upper range for white trainees. (2) For all groups there appeared to be significant foregone earnings as a result of the training process itself. These foregone earnings must be reckoned with in the calculation of the full social costs of training programs. (3) Despite considerable ambiguity of interpretation, training appeared to have increased the earnings of all trainee groups. (ASPER)

6.   Ashenfelter, Orley. Progress Report on the Development of Continuous Performance Information on the Impact of the Manpower Development and Training Act. Washington, D.C.: U.S. Department of Labor, 1973. NTIS PB268929/AS

This study describes progress during the first 2 years of development by the Office of the Assistant Secretary for Policy, Evaluation and Research (ASPER), of a continuous system for monitoring
the impact of Manpower Development and Training Act (MDTA) training
on trainee earnings. The basic system rests on matching: (1) data
on the characteristics of trainees from the information maintained
by the Office of Management Information Systems in the Manpower
Administration; and (2) information from the earnings records of
the Social Security Administration. The original results obtained
in 1972 from these data for the class of 1964 are described. These
preliminary results were based on faulty methodology; therefore,
improved results are also presented. It was found that the earnings of institutional trainees declined relative to the earnings of
the comparison group during 1964, when the enrollees were in
training. The average earnings of all 1964 MDTA trainee groups
were higher than they otherwise would have been over the period
1965-69. The effects of training on average earnings is seen to
vary with the race and sex of the trainee and the type of training
program. Preliminary calculations from more recent years suggest
that similar results may be obtained. The effects of training on
earnings were largest in the year immediately after training and
tended to decline thereafter. The study also extends the analysis
of MDTA trainees to later years and analyzed the effects of the
Work Incentive program, the Job Corps, and the Neighborhood Youth
Corps. (ASPER)

7.   Ashenfelter, Orley. The Effect of Manpower Training on Earnings:
Preliminary Results. Washington, D.C.: U.S. Department of Labor, 1975.
NTIS PB268815/AS

This research weighs the advantages and disadvantages of quantitative analysis of changes in earnings attributed to employment and
training programs, using longitudinal data on trainees from social
security records, and applies this method to one cohort of trainees
who participated in institutional (classroom) training under the
Manpower Development and Training Act (MDTA). Just as training was
considered the panacea of the 1960's for resolving the problems of
chronically unemployed workers, it is now widely believed that
these training programs were failures. Neither judgment about
training programs has been supported by any careful empirical
analysis. The earnings of the 1964 cohort of MDTA trainees studied
here did seem to have been raised by training above what they
otherwise would have been, though the absence of an experimental
design raises questions about the estimates. Clearly further work
with the data system described here would be desirable. Still,
there is no substitute for a carefully designed study using experimental methods, and there is no reason why this could not still be
carried out. But perhaps it is too late for such a study, given
the current emphasis on public employment programs. (ASPER)

8.   Autry, George B.   CETA Title VI Project Description Reports.
Volume I.   Chapel Hill, North Carolina: Manpower Development Corporation, 1977.   Volume II.   Washington, D.C.:   GPO, 1978.   NTIS PB268561/AS

The first volume in this two-part series describes in detail
approximately 50 successful CETA programs. It is designed to help

prime sponsors in using their funds under the President's economic stimulus program. The 50 projects represent activities of prime sponsors of varying type, size and geographical location.

Volume Two, prepared by the Employment and Training Administration in 1978, provides a description of 40 of the more than 50,000 new projects developed under the expansion efforts for Title VI. The formats adopted show a standard form outlining project title, prime sponsor type, project purpose and costs, and operating agency, followed by a summary description and an assessment of the project.

9.   Autry, George B. and R. C. Smith. The Planning and Implementation of CETA Title VI PSE Expansion Projects Under the Economic Stimulus Program of 1977. Chapel Hill, North Carolina: Manpower Development Corporation, 1977.

This study sheds light on the DOL/prime sponsors' dealings during the PSE buildup program phase. A number of significant policy areas are analyzed, e.g., the identification of PSE projects including the involvement of non-profit community-based organizations, the participation of the employment service and unemployment insurance agent, and the matching of CETA participants with veterans and welfare recipients. Manpower Development Corporation researchers concluded that despite the monetary delays, the uncertainty and confusion surrounding federal directives for prime sponsors, the expansion of the PSE program was relatively successful. Yet, there are still some areas for refinement in the present CETA system.

Volume Two, Detailed Findings, prepared by Manpower Development Corporation, provides a more detailed treatment of preparations that occurred in advance of actual program implementation, and includes sections dealing with federal guidance to prime sponsors, as well as the creation and utilization of pools of applicants eligible for PSE project proposals. It also discusses the state and local implementation experience, identifies factors that appeared to influence the speed of buildup, and assesses the results of the expansion in terms of jobs created and people served. An overview of research objectives and methods is included in the introduction to this volume.

10. Azzi, Corry F. Equity and Efficiency Effects from Manpower Programs. Lexington, Massachusetts: Lexington Books, 1973.

Employment and training programs established for the disadvantaged may have a range of complex objectives. Yet to be successful they must induce training and employment opportunities not being generated by market forces. The object of this study is to consider the process of investment in human capital in the behavior of firms and what role employment and training programs play in this process. A model is developed with two sets of conditions. The first distributes benefits primarily to the disadvantaged and the second distributed benefits primarily to the firm and shareholders. The hypothesis is that many programs mostly benefit firms and shareholders. This is tested for two large employers and the hypothesis confirmed.

11. Baily, Martin Neil and Robert M. Solow. "Public Service Employment as Macroeconomic Policy," in Job Creation Through Public Service Employment, Volume 3. Washington D.C.: National Commission for Manpower Policy, 1978. Y3.M31: 1/6/V.3

This paper presents a detailed discussion of unemployment and how macroeconomic policy operates to add to the aggregate demand for goods and services in order to draw unemployed labor and idle capacity into productive use.

The authors suggest that conventional expansionary policy measures differ from PSE as fiscal policy in that the former affects employment indirectly while the effects of the latter are direct.

A comparison between PSE with other expansionary fiscal policies is presented based on three main dimensions:
1. The purely aggregative or macroeconomic dimension.
2. The PSE intended side effects or objectives.
3. The PSE social goal--to avoid or diminish inflationary pressures.

It was found that the main disadvantages of PSE lie in the possibility of large-scale fiscal substitution and in the danger that PSE jobs will add very little to their holder's prospects of success in the traditional labor market.

It was determined that the main advantages of PSE in comparison with conventional fiscal policy lie in: (1) that it can be targeted to provide jobs for hard-to-employ groups in the labor force and for especially depressed cities and regions; (2) that PSE employment, correctly targeted, may be slightly less inflationary than the same amount of ordinary private sector employment so that total employment can safely be a little higher with a PSE component; and (3) that PSE can be coordinated with other forms of social insurance--public assistance and unemployment insurance for instance--to make them perhaps more effective and certainly more acceptable to public opinion.

Finally, the author suggests how to design and operate an effective PSE program in which both advantages and disadvantages are considered in order to be useful and effective.

12. Baily, Martin Neil and James Tobin. "Inflation-Unemployment Consequences of Job Creation Policies," in John Palmer (editor). Creating Jobs: Public Employment Programs and Wage Subsidies. Washington, D.C.: Brookings Institution, 1978, pp. 43-85.

The Baily-Tobin study provides an excellent and comprehensive analysis of the government's efforts in the area of public service employment (PSE) through direct job creation (DJC). Within the framework of the inflation-unemployment problem, the authors consider the issues of crowding out, bang for the buck (how much stimulus to GNP does one get from public service employment compared to alternative public expenditures?), and the effect on the Phillips curve. The analysis lends some credence to the belief

that DJC can diminish the inflationary by-products of unemployment
reductions in the short-run and can in the long-run permit monetary
and fiscal policies to aim at lower unemployment rates without so
tightening labor markets that inflation persistently accelerates.

13. Baily, Martin Neil and James Tobin. "Macroeconomic Effects of
Selective Public Employment and Wage Subsidies," Brookings Papers on
Economic Activity, 1977, pp. 511-54.

This paper presents an analytical discussion of empirical evidence
relating to the question of "Direct Job Creation, Inflation, and
Unemployment."

The authors present two analyses of the way selective employment
policies may work. The first is an aggregative model of frictional
unemployment and its possible reduction. The second is an expli-
citly disaggregated model of labor markets in which the power of
selective employment policies comes from exploiting differences
among markets in terms of wage responses. Consideration is given
to a basic strategy to reduce the natural rate of unemployment or
nonaccelerating inflation rate of unemployment (NAIRU).

The authors conclude that direct job creation, selective wage
subsidies or other labor-market policies depend on three hypotheses: (1) vacancies are independent of unemployment rates
(important for wage inflation); (2) primary unemployment of adult
males or of all adults is relatively more important for wage
behavior than unemployment of other workers; and (3) relative wage
levels affect adjustments of wages in specific markets or industries. The empirical evidence supports this conclusion although
the authors claim that in the long run displacement of workers from
private employment, both within and outside the target population,
will offset some of the direct employment gains.

14. Barnow, Burt S. Bias in the Estimates of the Treatment Effects in
Quasi-Experimental Evaluations. Washington, D.C.: U.S. Department of
Labor, 1977. NTIS PB280060/AS

This paper examines, in a formal analytical framework, some of the
conditions in which nonrandom selection procedures lead to bias in
estimation of treatment effects and the direction that such bias
takes. The goal of this paper is to demonstrate that in the
presence of measurement error for the independent variable, estimates of treatment effects may be biased. Both the magnitude and
direction of the bias are functions of the selection procedures
used and the relationship between the variables used in selection
and statistical control. The dangers of relying on an ad hoc rule
such as using the simple correlation between the control variable
and the treatment variable as an indicator of the direction the
bias will take are pointed out. The dangers of getting biased
estimates of treatment effect are likely to be present in quasi-
experimental evaluations of educational and employment programs.
Selection of control groups ex post from the untreated population
should be avoided. Planning the evaluation strategy at a program's
inception can minimize the likelihood of getting biased estimates
of the treatment effect. (ASPER)

15. Barocci, Thomas A. "The Canadian Job Creation Model and Its Applicability to the U.S.," in U.S. Congress, Joint Economic Committee, Achieving the Goals of the Employment Act of 1946-Thirtieth Anniversary Review, Volume I Employment. Paper No. 2. 93rd Congress, 1975. Y4.Ec7: Em 7/14

A discussion of the legal, philosophical and economic foundations of the Canadian job creation programs is followed by a brief evaluation of these programs. The primary emphasis of the paper addresses the issue of the applicability of the Canadian administrative provisions to the presently operating job creation programs in the United States, funded under the Comprehensive Employment and Training Act of 1973 (CETA). Specific attention is given to the problematic aspects of CETA and how these might be eliminated by incorporation of the Canadian "model" into CETA amendments or entirely new public jobs legislation. The analysis concludes with a positive, albeit qualified, recommendation for the adoption of the Canadian "model" in the United States. (JEL)

16. Barsby, Steve L. Cost-Benefit Analysis and Manpower Programs. Lexington, Massachusetts: D. C. Heath, 1972.

The application of cost-benefit analysis in the employment and training area is considered in this work. It looks at the various components of cost-benefit analysis with particular attention to the problems of estimating costs and benefits. The major portion of the book focuses on vocational education in secondary and post-secondary schools and on institutional out-of-school retraining under various state and federal programs. This second portion looks at State and Area/Redevelopment Act programs, Manpower Development and Training Act programs, and other programs such as the Neighborhood Youth Corps, Job Corps, and Work Experience and Training Program.

17. Battelle, Peter E. The Development of a System for Financial Management of Public Service Employment Subcontracts: The Vermont Experience. Montpelier, Vermont: Vermont State Employment Service, 1973. NTIS PB232180/0GI

The most difficult problem in the financial management of a Public Service Employment program (or subsidized work-training experience) is the over-obligation of funds. Some training slots are never filled, some trainees drop out early from the program, and others complete their training early. All of these factors "free" funds, which must be promptly identified if they are to be put to alternative uses. The best way to avoid this problem is to use a detailed and flexible working budget kept up to date by timely and systematic comparison between actual and projected expenditures. The central office should use actual rather than anticipated outlays as a means of controlling costs. Realistic allowance should also be made for delays in employer billings. (NTIS)

18. Baumer, Donald C.; Carl E. Van Horn; and Mary Marvel. "Explaining Benefit Distribution in CETA Programs," Journal of Human Resources, 14, Spring, 1979, pp. 171-196.

Using data from a three-year study of CETA in 32 research sites, this article describes and analyzes the distribution of benefits to individuals from CETA programs. The data shows that the poor and women receive fewer benefits from CETA, while nonwhites experience higher enrollment under CETA than under noncategorical programs. The poor, the women, and nonwhites obtain fewer benefits from Public Service Employment programs than from training and work experience programs. Economic conditions provide only a partial explanation of service patterns. Program design choices, administrator attitudes, national policies and actions are also important. Some changes are recommended in methods of analyzing the need for employment and training programs. (ERIC)

19. Betsey, Charles L., et al. CETA Reauthorization Issues. Washington, D.C.: Congressional Budget Office, 1978. Y10.0: C73/2

This background paper analyzes current CETA public service employment programs and other Federal manpower programs for the economically disadvantaged. The authors attempt to measure the impact of eligibility and funding changes proposed under H.R. 11086, the CETA reauthorization bill, and related bills S. 2570 and H.R. 12452. The Appendix contains selected FY77 tabular data on CETA program participation and expenditures. (CIS)

20. Bloch, Farrell E. (editor). Evaluating Manpower Training Programs: Revisions on Papers Originally Presented at the Conference on Evaluating Manpower Training Programs. Greenwich, Connecticut,: JAI Press, 1979.

This report consists of ten previously unpublished papers plus comments concerning the evaluation of changes in earnings of participants in the manpower training programs and examining the problems of comparing earnings of a nonparticipating control group. Papers cover the selection of a sample size, the appropriateness of the control group, difficulties of modeling and evaluation study, evaluation of econometric analyses of the economic benefits of specific programs, and labor market displacement effects. Also included are analyses of Markov Process Models and the estimation of production functions in manpower programs.

21. Borus, Michael E. Evaluating the Impact of Manpower Programs. Washington, D.C.: U.S. Department of Labor, 1971. NTIS PB255315/AS

This report contains the papers presented at a 1971 conference on the evaluation of manpower programs. Some 20 papers deal with various aspects of 7 topics: (1) designing an evaluation system; (2) the choice of appropriate control groups; (3) designing survey instruments; (4) measuring the noneconomic impacts (on health, education, crime, and the community) of manpower programs; (5) finding the hard-to-locate; (6) sources of economic data in manpower evaluation studies; and (7) measuring secondary labor market effects of manpower programs. (ASPER)

22. Borus, Michael E. "Indicators of CETA Performance," Industrial and Labor Relations Review, 32, October, 1978, pp. 3-14.

Prime sponsors under the Comprehensive Employment and Training Act of 1973 (CETA) need to evaluate the performance of different types of manpower services provided by different service deliverers. This study attempts to validate 19 proxies that have been used as indicators of long-run program impact--such as employment status, hours worked, and weekly earnings 30 days after leaving the program. The results indicate that none of the indicators tested were strongly correlated with success in CETA programs. The author concludes that continued use of these indicators will yield allocation decisions that are little better, if at all, than those made by flipping a coin. (ILRR)

23. Borus, Michael E. Measuring The Impact of Employment Related Social Programs. Kalamazoo, Michigan: Upjohn Institute for Employment Research, 1979.

This work is a revised version of Measuring the Impact of Manpower Programs: A Primer written by Michael E. Borus and William R. Tash with changes being based on developments in the field in the ten years following the publication of the initial work. In this latest volume, the author offers an approach and a methodology for the systematic measurement of the impact of employment related social programs. Its primary emphasis is on basic evaluation techniques, with references to numerous theoretical and conceptual issues. It is intended to assist those who conduct impact evaluations and program planners and administrators who must make decisions based on these evaluations. Topics covered are: the impact of social programs, evaluation design, the costs of social programs, and combining the measures of program impact and cost.

24. Borus, Michael E. and Charles G. Buntz. "Problems and Issues in the Evaluation of Manpower Programs," Industrial and Labor Relations Review, 25, January, 1972, pp. 234-245.

A review of techniques for the evaluation of manpower programs reveals not only significant progress over the past decade but also many areas in which the methodology is still inadequate to yield reliable answers to policy questions. Among the latter are the determination of the program unit for study, the choice of the control group, the selection of variables to measure program effectiveness, cost calculations, the measurement of secondary effects of programs, and long-run projections of benefits. This paper details the issues in each area. (ILRR)

25. Borus, Michael E. and Daniel S. Hamermesh. "Estimating Fiscal Substitution by Public Service Employment Programs," Journal of Human Resources, 13, Fall, 1978, pp. 561-565.

This article is a short comment on a paper by Johnson and Tomola entitled "The Fiscal Substitution Effect of Alternative Approaches to Public Service Employment Policy" published in the Journal of Human Resources, Winter 1977, pp. 3-26 (#98). It suggests changes in methodology and policy to clarify some of the results of the Johnson and Tomola paper. (ERIC)

26. Borus, Michael E. and Daniel S. Hamermesh. "Study of the Net Employment Effects of Public Service Employment: Econometric Analyses" in Job Creation Through Public Service Employment, Volume 3. Washington, D.C.: National Commission for Manpower Policy, 1978. Y3.M31: 1/6/V.3

> Borus and Hamermesh present a review of various econometric studies conducted by other professionals in the field in order to determine the effectiveness of PSE in reaching two main objectives: (1) to increase the aggregate national employment; and (2) to increase employment in the communities to which funds are allocated. This concern arose from three econometric studies appearing in 1974: "Public Employment Programs: An Evaluative Study" by Alan E. Fechter; "An Impact Evaluation of the Public Employment Program" by George E. Johnson and James D. Tomola; and "An Evaluation of the Economic Impact Project of the Public Employment Program" by the National Planning Association. Each of the studies concluded that grantees were using part of the PSE funds in the place of their own revenues to hire individuals for jobs that would have been filled in the absence of the PSE programs, a phenomenon known as the fiscal substitution effect.
>
> Several econometric studies are reviewed with the question of fiscal substitution as the central issue. None of the studies were found to provide a satisfactory estimate of the degree to which PSE induces fiscal substitution. The studies present a widely varying estimate of the net job creation effects of PSE depending on the assumptions, specifications, and data use. As a result, the authors suggest that the use of alternative techniques--surveys and the stationing of professional observers--combined with econometric techniques, will produce a more satisfactory answer to the job creation and fiscal substitution question. Finally, this paper concludes that econometric analysis can be useful in estimating the fiscal substitution effect and the broader issues of use of funds and aggregate effects if it is properly designed and used in conjunction with other evaluative techniques.

27. Borus, Michael E. and William E. Tash. Measuring the Impact of Manpower Programs: A Primer. Ann Arbor, Michigan: Institute of Labor and Industrial Relations, 1972.

> See abstract under Borus, Michael E. Measuring the Impact of Employment Related Social Programs (#22).

28. Briggs, Vernon M., Brian Rungeling and Lewis H. Smith. "Public Service Employment in the Rural South: The Prospects for Job Transition," IRRA 32nd Annual Proceedings, 1979, pp. 195-202.

> Public Service programs in eight counties from the states of Georgia and Mississippi were studied with particular attention directed to the question of job transition. The study finds that program outcomes conform to standard labor market theory except that the probability of transition declines with length of time in a PSE job. This is the result of the submersion of the transition goal resulting from the expansion of PSE as a countercylical tool with the result that program delivery agents do not consider transition to be an important local objective. When combined with

the relatively few job openings in the private sector, less potential for transition exists. Thus, this paper concludes that lower
transition potential, the characteristics of eligible populations
and local economic conditions demand more than a temporary policy
if the quality of life in the rural South is to improve.

29. Bromley, James and Larry Wordle. On the Job Training: CETA
Program Models. Washington, D.C.: Employment and Training Administration, 1978. L37.8/6: On 1/978

On the Job Training (OJT) is reviewed to provide CETA prime sponsors and OJT program operators with information and direction. The
monograph is more than a technical guide in that it presents an
overview of the philosophy and operations of OJT for both policy
makers and program operators. It considers the strengths, weaknesses, and limitations of OJT as well as its conflicting objectives. The monograph argues for further utilization of private
sector employees in OJT programs through policies such as incentive
payments, variable reimbursement rates and contract extension. It
concludes with an evaluation of OJT and its application under CETA
and makes recommendations for program improvements.

30. Bruno, Lee. Intake and Assessment: CETA Program Models. Washington, D.C.: Employment and Training Administration, 1978. L37.8/6: In8

The intake and assessment of clients for employment and training
programs is the focus of this report. It examines the various
elements in the process and how they interact. Based on an understanding of the process, the report reviews assessment techniques
available for use by programs. Variations of program models are
discussed and the impacts of various combinations on programs
demonstrated. Case studies of current CETA prime sponsor applica-
tions are reviewed.

31. Burleson, Erica. The Role of the Coach in Public Service Employment: The Vermont Experience, Final Report. Montpelier, Vermont:
Vermont State Employment Service, 1973. NTIS TB231 898/8GI

This report describes on a firsthand basis the role played by the
"coach" in the Vermont Experimental and Demonstration Manpower
pilot project. The paraprofessional coach, or "employment service
aide," acts as a client advocate who helps the client adjust to a
work environment. As one part of a three member employability
team, the coach's duties begin after the client has been accepted
for placement in a special work training situation. Constant
communication is maintained until the client's barriers to employability are overcome. Responsibilities of the coach vary from
acquainting the program enrollee with simulated interviews to
helping resolve family friction which may hinder the individual's
effectiveness. (ERIC)

32. Butler, T. Wendell and Richard Hobbie. Employment and Training
Programs. Washington, D.C.: Congressional Budget Office, 1976. Y10.2:
Em 7/2

This staff working paper was prepared for the House Budget Commit-tee's Human Resource Task Force and covers unemployment and employ-ment policies. In particular, it focuses on the range of Federal employment and training programs available to reduce unemployment, increase job opportunities, and improve worker skills. The analysis considers such factors as client characteristics, program costs and effects, and policy alternatives. (CIS)

33. Casey, Florence M. (editor). Perspectives on Public Job Creation. Washington, D.C.: Employment and Training Administration, 1977. L37.14:52

Perspectives on Public Job Creation is an anthology of papers by academicians and other experts in which the job creation potential of a major public jobs program is explored from a diversity of viewpoints. The twelve contributing authors were encouraged to adopt a relatively free-wheeling approach to the issue in order to elicit the greatest possible number of ideas. They were also asked to estimate the employment impact of different approaches to the problem of creating public jobs. As a result, some of the projects described or suggested in the papers may not be feasibly undertaken at the present time for legal or practical reasons (e.g., certain statutory restrictions on wage subsidies for jobs in the private sector under the CETA Act of 1973 or certain railroad rehabilita-tion projects). Prime sponsors should, therefore, consider the legal as well as the practical feasibility of any projects dis-cussed in this monograph. Nevertheless, the authors have identified a large number of potential targets for job creation projects in a wide range of occupations and industries. There are several ideas discussed which could be adapted to suit the needs and resources of individual areas and which could be extremely useful to prime sponsors, who are seeking ways to implement new programs in their respective jurisdictions.

34. Cashman, John R. and Robert E. Mattson. Long Term Follow-Through of Participants in the Vermont Experimental and Demonstration Project. Montpelier, Vermont: Vermont State Employment Service, 1974. NTIS PB-241-224/5GI

The report describes a Vermont project begun in 1970 and designed to assess the long-term value of the Special Work Project (SWP), or Public Service Employment, as a vehicle for providing transitional employment to unemployed members of low income families with children receiving public aid. The study attempted to contact and interview the 609 participants who had completed or terminated special work training prior to June, 1973, in order to determine their employment status and public aid recipient status at 9, 12, 18, 24, and 30 months subsequent to SWP. At each follow-through contact, completers were more likely to be employed than were terminators (69% of completers versus 44% of terminators). Among all 486 trainees located and interviewed, there was a significant decrease in persons receiving public assistance (from 58% to 32%) between the time of entry into SWP training and the follow-through contact nine months subsequent to training. The study also des-cribes hourly wage, experience, overtime, types of employment, characteristics of trainees, and trainee's perception of project

value. Twenty-two detailed tables are included and additional
project data is appended. (NTIS)

35. Ciscel, David and Barbara Tuckman, "The Peripheral Worker: CETA
Training As Imperfect Job Socialization," Journal of Economic Issues,
15, June, 1981, pp. 489-500.

The objective of this study is to evaluate the influence of the
CETA experience in the post-program work history of the CETA
trainee. Its methodology is based on a combination of two
approaches: case study and survey, and tested using data from
Tennessee CETA programs. Because the economically disadvantaged do
not follow a standard work history, the study examines weaknesses
in individuals' education, training and job experiences to determine the remedial assistance provided by the CETA program and its
impact in modifying the behavior of the peripheral workers. The
CETA experience and the post-training labor market experience of
the trainees is evaluated in terms of aggregate measures of change
(e.g. earnings, employment stability, dependence and attitudes
towards the job market). This approach is innovative in that it
links the CETA program to the behavior of the CETA participants.
Three types of trainees were identified as a result of this study:
the labor market failures; those who came to CETA as an employer of
last resort; and the breakthroughs or successful participants. The
three groups differ in relation to their maturity and labor market
awareness with the breakthroughs seeing CETA as the key to their
work history transformation while the other two types did not.

36. Congressional Budget Office and National Commission for Employment
Policy. CETA Training Programs – Do They Work for Adults? Washington,
D.C.: Congressional Budget Office and National Commission for Employ-
ment Policy, 1982. Y10.2:C73/3

To provide background information on the issues of who is to be
served and what services are to be provided by employment and
training programs, this report analyzes the effects of CETA training on participants' post-program earnings. CETA provided services
include classroom training, on-the-job training, work experience
and job search and placement assistance. The first three elements
are generally short-term (lasting about 20 weeks per participant)
and, in 1980, cost an average of $2,400 per participant. Analysis
of information on persons over 24 years of age who entered a CETA
program in fiscal year 1976 indicate that training increased the
average future earnings of female participants substantially but
did not seem to affect the average future earnings of male participants. Those with the least past employment experience had the
largest post-training earnings gains. Based on these findings the
report discusses the issues to be faced in redesigning employment
and training programs and comments on the alternative legislation
being proposed.

37. Corpus, Ray E., Jr. Public Service Employment: CETA Program
Models. Washington, D.C.: Employment and Training Administration,
1978. L37.816: P96

The intent of this monograph is to explore, from the perspective of practitioners attempting to implement or redesign PSE programs, three major approaches to PSE: countercyclical, employability development and structural targeting. The content is presented in six sections. The first briefly presents the historical development of PSE, while section two presents a typology of PSE involving three dimensions: objectives, target groups and employment opportunity. Each of the next three sections discusses these three dimensions in relation to one model for approaching PSE. The three models covered are: the countercyclical model (create jobs in the public sector); the employability development model (provide job training); and the structural targeting model (select a target group and deal specifically with their unemployment problems). The last section discusses some unresolved PSE issues.

38. Craft, James A. Public Service Jobs and Transitional Employment: An Analysis of the Vermont Experimental and Demonstration Project. Washington, D.C.: U.S. Department of Labor, 1974. NTIS PB-236 183/0ST

The three year E&D Project in Vermont using subsidized Public Service Employment to provide transitional work experience for low-income unemployed and welfare recipients is described and analyzed. A conceptual model of the transition process is developed and operationalized for measurement. Analysis of the data indicates a relatively high transition rate for clients in the Program. The clients who transitioned had good job retention and welfare reduction results compared to those not transitioning. PSE appears to be most useful as a channel or mechanism to obtain steady primary labor market employment and seems to be most effective with clients who have better labor market experiences and/or shorter welfare histories. (ERIC)

39. Crandall, R. W., C. Duncan MacRae, and L. Y. L. Yap. Employment and Wage Effects of the WIN Tax Credit. Washington, D.C.: U.S. Department of Labor, 1972. NTIS PB253586/AS

In this study, the Work Incentive (WIN) tax credit was described and a procedure for calculating the effective subsidy rate was provided, based on a hypothesis of the operation of the tax-credit in low-skill labor markets. The study reviewed an econometric analysis of the market for low-skill labor and provided estimates of the effect of the WIN tax credit for 1973. It was concluded that while neither the WIN tax credit nor the WIN program alone could generate a significant increase in employment among recipients of Aid to Families with Dependent Children without displacing other low-skill workers, a combination of these programs could. (ASPER)

40. Dachler, Peter. Persons and Organization Characteristics Involved in CETA Program Effectiveness: Issues in Need of Research. Washington, D.C.: U.S. Department of Labor, 1979. NTIS PB298137/AS

Based upon a general literature review on CETA organizational research, as well as upon selected interviews conducted in a few ongoing CETA programs, Federal agencies, potential employers of CETA participants, and State employment service agencies, research issues regarding the organizational characteristics of CETA organizations and characteristics of their members are identified in this work. Research issues at the interorganizational, organizational, inter- and intro- group, and the individual level of analysis are discussed with respect to their potential impact on CETA organizational effectiveness. Special emphasis is placed on different perspectives of CETA organization effectiveness that are required for an analysis of personal and organizational characteristics in CETA organizations. This report ends with a brief discussion of methodological and research approach issues that are implied by the main arguments of this paper. (ASPER)

41. Dimmit, M. and E. Renshaw. "A Note on the Government Employment Multiplier," Nebraska Journal of Economics, 16, Summer, 1977, pp. 47-56.

Dimmit and Renshaw provide a public policy overview of PSE. The authors point out that it is difficult to imagine how a condition of reasonably full employment can be achieved in the near future without an expanded program of public service employment. They discuss conventional multipliers, which emphasize income rather than employment effects, being used in the furthering of stabilization theory and policy and how such multipliers have failed to explain employment change. Employment multiplier models are presented and analyzed assuming that a hypothesis must be formed about the behavior of employment before deriving the employment multipliers. The analysis begins by noting that the changes in total employment can be separated into various components, such as: (1) the change in government employment; (2) the change in employment in durable goods industries; (3) the change in construction employment; and (4) the change in employment in other industries. By assuming that the change in other employment will be a simple linear function of the change in the remaining sectors, a multiplier relationship is obtained to explain employment change.

42. Director, Steven. Underadjustment Bias in the Evaluation of Manpower Training. Washington, D.C.: U.S. Department of Labor, 1976. NTIS PB270525/AS

In the absence of randomization in evaluations of employment and training programs, one cannot assume pretraining equivalence between trainees and the control group. The problem then becomes to "adjust away" any pretraining differences, so that the post-training differences can be validly interpreted as an estimate of the training's effect. This study argues that the usual evaluation designs systematically underadjust for pretraining differences and hence produce biased results. The study's objectives were: (1) to clarify the source of underadjustment bias: (2) to survey the literature and suggest the probable direction of this bias present in the major evaluations; (3) to investigate whether such biases can plausibly be of sufficient magnitude to alter the policy implications of evaluation results; and (4) to investigate the feasibility of statistically correcting for such biases. The findings suggest that while bias often distorts evaluation results, a valid correction can be made only when a number of specific assumptions are satisfied. Given the uncertainty of these assumptions, the basic recommendation is to increase the use of randomized experiments in program evaluation. (ASPER)

43. Doeringer, Peter B. (editor). <u>Workplace Perspectives on Education and Training</u>. Boston, Massachusetts: Martinus Nijhoff, 1981.

The relationship between education and work with particular attention to the role of the workplace as a training ground for workers in the U.S. economy is addressed in this volume. If we are to effectively coordinate public employment and training policies with private sector workplace policies, knowledge of both the operation of the workplace training system and the incentives guiding the decisions of employers and workers is required. The essays in this volume present estimates of workplace training cost, the extent of training being provided and the types of training available. Perspectives on workplace training are provided for the national level, in the experience of particular employers (Bell and Xerox), for the public sector and in situations involving regulated and unionized occupations.

44. Dow, Gregory. <u>Cost Analysis of CETA</u>. Washington, D.C.: U.S. Department of Labor, 1977. NTIS PB282971/AS

This study estimates functions relating expenditures and enrollments for programs funded under the Comprehensive Employment and Training Act (CETA) using data from the fiscal 1976 quarterly reports of CETA prime sponsors to the Employment and Training Administration (Quarterly Progress Reports, Financial Status Reports, and Program Summaries, and the Quarterly Summaries of Participant Characteristics). A model of CETA enrollments and expenditures is developed and estimated using a production function framework. The inputs to the training process are taken to be expenditures on marketed inputs as well as the characteristics of trainees. Such functions are statistically estimated. The marginal costs of enrollment in various programs are estimated on the basis of these results, and the model's predictive accuracy is assessed. (ASPER)

45. Dunning, Bruce B. <u>Post-training Outcomes: Experiences with the Portland WIN Voucher Training Program.</u> Washington, D.C.: Bureau of Social Science Research, Inc., 1977.

Vouchers for vocational training were tested in Portland, Oregon. The post-training labor force and welfare experiences of WIN participants who received vouchers which allowed them greater freedom and responsibility for making and acting on decisions concerning their skill training is compared with the experiences of earlier WIN participants who received conventional WIN training. The results indicate that voucher recipients were slightly less likely to be consistently in the labor force than regular WIN participants. However, the voucher recipients were more likely to be totally free of welfare and when on welfare to have lower levels of support than regular WIN participants. This report concludes that vouchering was feasible in Portland. But, while results were encouraging, changes accompanying vouchering were marginal.

46. Ehrenberg, Ronald G. "Heterogeneous Labor, Minimum Hiring Standards, and Job Vacancies in Public Employment," <u>Journal of Political Economy</u>, 81, November/December, 1973, pp. 1442-1450.

The author of this study presents an alternative explanation for the persistent and widespread job vacancies or shortages among public employees. He is critical of the assumption that "local governments can be considered monopsonists in the markets for job classes for which they are large employers" and presents a model of the public employee wage-vacancy relationship to explain and to support this position.

The model is used to explain variations in vacancy rates among police departments in a sample of over 400 United States cities in 1967. The evidence indicates that, contrary to the implication derived from the textbook monopsony model, increasing the wages of public employees, a priori, would not necessarily prove to be an effective means of reducing job vacancies.

47. Ehrenberg, Ronald G. and James G. Hewlett. The Impact of the WIN II Program on Welfare Cost and Recipient Rates. Washington, D.C.: U.S. Department of Labor, 1974. NTIS PB256907/AS

This paper presents an econometric analysis of the impact of the Work Incentive (WIN) Program, as modified by the Talmadge Admendments of 1971 (WIN II), on Aid to Families with Dependent Children (AFDC) program costs and recipient rates. Estimating the macroeconomic impact of the program requires first a model of how these welfare cost variables would vary over time in the absence of the WIN II program. Many of the variables used in previous studies exhibit little short-run intertemporal variability over the 18-month span of the program within a State and are omitted from this analysis. The simple model presented by Johnson and Reed (#98) is expanded to consider the impact of WIN II placements on benefits and the average benefit level per family. The model is estimated separately for a number of periods since the WIN II program began, to observe how its impacts vary over time. A test is made of whether the mix of services provided program participants influences the size of program effects, and several other extensions of the analysis are discussed. The program's impact on AFDC costs is found not to be substantial and varied over time. The evidence indicates that welfare costs have been reduced only for those WIN II placements who also receive some type of training. Consequently, although the data are subject to large measurement errors and the estimating equations are perhaps too simplistic, it is suggested that concentration on the program's placement function, to the total exclusion of the training function, is probably a misallocation of resources. (ASPER)

48. Farnell, James E. and Elaine Pitzalis. "How Welfare Recipients Find Jobs: A Case Study in New Jersey," Monthly Labor Review, 101, February, 1978, pp. 43-45.

This short article on the effectiveness of various government programs in placing unemployed in jobs, compares WIN, CETA, NJES, and EATS among themselves and then as a group (government) to alternative private methods, such as friends or newspapers. "Of all methods, the Comprehensive Employment and Training Act (CETA) and Civil Service examinations grouped together were the most effective; their success rate was 83 percent." The study was done

by the Monmouth County Welfare Board, Monmouth County, New Jersey.
(ERIC)

49. Fechter, Alan E. Public Employment Programs. Washington, D.C.:
American Enterprise Institute, 1975.

This monograph discusses the objectives and performance of public
employment and determines that much depends on the amount of
displacement which takes place. In considering the issue of
displacement an analytic framework is developed and the evidence to
date on total expenditure displacement, wage-bill expenditure
displacement, and net employment effects is presented. The author
then considers the human capital effects and employment effects for
target groups of the Neighborhood Youth Corps, Public Service
Careers, Operation Mainstream and Public Employment Program.

50. Fechter, Alan E. Public Service Employment: Boon or Boondoggle?
Washington, D.C.: Urban Institute, 1975.

The role of Public Service Employment (PSE) programs as a means of
coping with periods of recession is examined in this monograph.
Toward this end, the objectives of PSE programs are outlined and
the evidence relating to the achievement of such programs is
reviewed. Because the actual impact of PSE programs is often quite
different from the expected and because the actual impact is at
times undesirable, the author questions the role of PSE as a
countercyclical policy tool. In addition, PSE as a more general
policy tool is discussed in light of the empirical results.

51. Fechter, Alan E. and Laurie Bassi. The Implications for Fiscal
Substitution and Occupational Displacement Under an Expanded CETA Title
VI.   Washington,   D.C.:   U.S.   Department   of   Labor,   1979.   NTIS
PB292497/AS

The purpose of this study is to provide evidence on the efficacy of
the expanded Comprehensive Employment and Training Act Public
Service Employment (CETA PSE) programs as a means of reducing
unemployment in a noninflationary way. The study consists of: (1)
a review of existing literature; (2) the development of appropriate
analytic models; and (3) empirical analyses aimed at providing
information on fiscal substitution.

The empirical analysis is limited to estimating the fiscal substitution effects of CETA, estimating the effects of CETA on the
functional distribution of local government employment, and estimating the effects of CETA on wage rates of local government
employees. (ASPER)

52. Finifter, David H. An Analysis of Differential Earnings Paths of
CETA Participants and CPS Matched Comparison Groups. Williamsburg,
Virginia: College of William and Mary, 1982.

An analysis of the pattern of earnings of CETA participants entering adult-oriented programs in fiscal year 1976 compared to the
patterns for their matched comparison groups derived from the 1976
CPS is presented in this paper. Using a number of alternative

econometric methods and a conceptual framework of the transmission mechanism involved in CETA participation including skill enhancement, improved labor market contacts and employment experience on the job, the study finds that earnings impacts differ widely across program activities and participant subgroups with the estimates being neither uniformly positive nor large.

53. Finifter, David H. An Analysis of Two Year Post-Program Earnings Paths of CETA Participants Using Early CLMS Cohorts. Washington, D.C.: Employment and Training Administration, 1980. NTIS PB81-155525/AS

The study uses the initial two cohorts of the Continuous Longitudinal Manpower Survey (CLMS) to examine the earnings paths of persons who enrolled in adult-oriented Comprehensive Employment and Training Act (CETA) programs during the first six months of 1975. By using a pooled cross-section/time series data structure and multiple regression, earnings patterns from the fourth quarter prior to entry through the eighth quarter after termination are examined. Although it cannot be attributed to program participation, one overall pattern stood out among the several identified: post-program earnings paths moved upward and there is no fall back to pre-program levels. (NTIS)

54. Finifter, David H. Pre- and Post-Program Labor Supply Behavior of CETA Participants: An Analysis of Labor Force Attachment. Williamsburg, Virginia: College of William and Mary, 1982.

This paper analyzes the question of labor supply behavior of employment and training program participants using fiscal year 1976 cohorts from the CLMS. The study focuses on the probability that an individual participates in the labor market and the number of weeks an individual is in the labor force in the year prior to entry into a CETA program and in each of the first two post-program years.

Using logit to estimate the labor force participant equation and Tobit to estimate the weeks in the labor force equation, Finifter finds that the proportion of CETA terminees who participated in the labor force in the pre-program year was high (91% for males and 82% for females) and these proportions rose during the first post-program year while dropping during the second post-program year to a level slightly below the pre-program level. In addition, weeks in the labor force increase substantially between the pre-program and first post-program year and show either a sustained level or an increase between the first and second post-program year.

55. Frank, R. H. Public Service Employment and the Supply of Labor to the Private Sector. Berkeley, California: Institute of Industrial Relations, 1971. NTIS PB-244 453/1

This study assesses the impact of large scale public service employment on private labor markets. Because serious flaws in existing labor supply studies compromise their usefulness as tools for assessing public service employment impacts, the author develops a model which eliminates many of the problems. Using data from the Survey of Economic Opportunity, the model is estimated for several demographic subgroups. The results indicate substantial wage elasticity of supply for almost all subgroups. As a result, the author concludes that the expansion of public service employment considered at the time would not produce serious dislocations in private labor markets.

56. Galchick, Janet and Michael Wiseman. "Subsidizing Employment in the Nonprofit Sector," in Richard P. Nathan, Robert F. Cook and V. Lane Rawlins. Public Service Employment: A Field Evaluation. Washington, D.C.: Brookings Institution, 1981.

In 1977 the Carter administration's economic stimulus package attempted to use nonprofit organizations on a large scale to produce public service employment jobs. This study discusses the various aspects of the movement toward using nonprofit organization and their role in CETA job creation efforts. The outcome of an analysis of the experience in San Francisco is reported with the conclusion that important behavioral differences exist among different types of nonprofit organizations and that these differences affect performance under CETA-PSE. Information from field associates in the Brookings PSE study (#164) was also analyzed with the conclusion that these reports generally support the conclusions drawn from the San Francisco analysis.

57. Garfinkel, Irwin and John Palmer. "Issues, Evidences, and Implications," in John Palmer (editor). Creating Jobs: Public Employment Programs and Wage Subsidies. Washington, D.C.: Brookings Institution, 1978, pp. 1-42.

Irwin Garfinkel and John Palmer present an overview of the current state of knowledge of direct job creating policies. The first two sections address questions revelant to the objectives of achieving and sustaining higher levels of employment without excessive inflationary pressure. In particular they discuss whether direct job creation policies are superior to more conventional alternatives for reducing cyclical unemployment and how capable they are of reducing structural unemployment. The third section focuses on the microeconomic efficiency of public employment programs and compares their efficiency with that of income maintenance programs. The authors conclude that both public employment programs and wage subsidies have significant advantages and disadvantages for dealing with structural unemployment but until more is learned about them, the scale on which they eventually might operate effectively is highly uncertain. There appears to be no general reason to greatly prefer one approach over the other although one may have more potential effectiveness than the other for particular target groups.

58. Garvin, Charles D., Audrey D. Smith and William J. Reid. The Work Incentive Experience. Montclair, New Jersey: Allanheld, Osmun and Co., 1978.

This study is the result of a four-year research program by faculty and staff of the Schools of Social Work at the University of Chicago, University of Michigan, and Case Western Reserve University. The focus of the research is the Work Incentive Program with the major objective of demonstrating how individuals enrolled in the WIN program were affected both during and after participation in the program. The thirteen chapters include: The Study of WIN Careers, Forty Years of Work Training, WIN Research: A Review of the Findings, Three Studies of WIN, A Gallery of WIN Portraits, The Organization of WIN and Its Impact on Participants, Hope for a Better Life, The Carrot and the Stick, Experiences in the Work Incentive Program, Child Care, Eighteen Months Later, Toward a Consumer- Oriented Program, and Directions for WIN.

59. Gay, Robert S. and Michael E. Borus. "Validating Performance Indicators for Employment and Training Programs," Journal of Human Resources, 15, Winter, 1980, pp. 29-48.

Proxies are used to indicate the impact of employment and training programs. CETA prime sponsors and the Labor Department rely on these performance indicators for fund allocations. This study correlates eight indicators with the impact on earnings of participants in four types of programs. The study shows that performance indicators presently being used, which are primarily constructed from placement data, provide no useful information for judging relative program effectiveness. Other indicators, particularly changes in weeks in the labor force, weeks employed, and wage rates, while far from perfect, are correlated much more with earnings gain. (JHR)

60. Gayer, Gordon, et al. The Use of Training Related Expense and Enrichment Monies in Public Service Employment. The Vermont Experience. Montpelier, Vermont: Vermont Department of Employment Security, 1973. NTIS PB-232 211/3

The necessity of having funds which meet client work related and additional educational needs are presented in this two-part monograph. The first part is comprised of a comprehensive discussion of Training Related Expenses and an analysis of their uses and effects on client completion or termination from training. The second part describes the function and utilization of Enrichment Training. Conclusions drawn from both parts are that these funds are valuable tools and have a real and positive impact on the success of clients requiring this type of help. (NTIS)

61. Geraci, Vincent. Preliminary Evaluation of MIS for CETA. Washington, D.C.: U.S. Department of Labor, 1978. NTIS PB287333/AS

This report is the documentation of Public Use Version of the Continuous Wage and Benefit History (CWBH) tapes. The Arizona Employment and Unemployment Data Set (AZEUD) is made up of information drawn from administrative records of government agencies in two separate samples: (1) A 20-percent sample of workers who applied for unemployment insurance (UI) in Arizona from 1963 to 1971, and (2) 1-percent sample of the Arizona labor force from 1957 to 1972. The 20-percent sample is drawn from the Continuous Wage and Benefit History (CWBH) data maintained by the Arizona Bureau of Employment Security. This data base contains detailed longitudinal histories of both the employment and unemployment experience of workers who claimed UI benefits in Arizona from 1963 to 1971. About 40,000 workers are included in the file. The 1-percent sample is derived from the Social Security Administration's Longitudinal Employee-Employer Data (LEED) file. The data base contains detailed longitudinal histories of the employment experience of workers covered by Social Security employed in Arizona from 1957 to 1973. There is no explicit indicator of whether or not workers in this sample claimed unemployment insurance. About 25,000 workers are included in this file. The data are contained on two reels of magnetic tape. The data tapes are 9 track, EDCBIC, 1600 bpi, with standard labels suitable for use with IBM and most other computers. (ASPER)

62. Gibbons, Christina. The Role of the Counselor in Public Service Employment: The Vermont Experience. Final Report. Montpelier, Vermont: Vermont State Employment Service, 1973. NTIS TB232 048/9GI

A counselor's presents a first-hand account of her experience with Vermont's Manpower pilot project on Public Service Employment. This statewide project was designed to test temporary subsidized employment in nonprofit agencies for low income clients. The report describes and refers to many case studies, specifically, those who entered the program because they were liable for the support of children, and also had no or low income. Although the program originally was committed toward helping "hardcore unemployables," emphasis was shifted to those who evidenced fewer, less severe barriers to employment. Clients were placed in subsidized employment for 6 months, with the expectation that their work experience would lead to permanent nonsubsidized employment. The counselor devoted her energies to help the client overcome major barriers for employment, such as: transportation, child care, and job attitude. (ERIC)

63. Ginzberg, Eli. Good Jobs, Bad Jobs, No Jobs. Cambridge, Massachusetts: Harvard University Press, 1979.

This text addresses the complexities of the job problem—more seekers than jobs—and the national efforts to ameliorate the problem. The aim of the book is to provide background and understanding about the changes that are occurring in the number and types of jobs available in the U.S. economy and the parallel changes that are underway in the characteristics of job seekers.

Part one, "People and Jobs," provides a framework within which the job problem must be considered and solved. It is a framework that should bound most discussions of employment, unemployment, and income by delineating recent changes in the structure of the American family and the changing role of women. Basic data is provided for the longer view: How well has the U.S. economy performed with respect to job creation since WWII, with respect to the total number of new jobs as well as the growth of "good jobs"? The prospects of the nation reaching full employment within the next few years is considered.

Part two, "Education and Work," focuses on "trained manpower," i.e., how newcomers to an urban environment acquire jobs and competence, the outlook for college graduates, a short and longer run assessment of the supply and demand for managerial personnel, and a section on professionals, managers, and the establishment.

Part three, "Manpower Planning and Policy," presents three dimensions of the manpower planning and policy process. The first is a focus on the opportunities and difficulties facing large organizations in their attempts to manage their human resources. The second is the issue of assuring an adequate supply of competent manpower in a modern nation and what role apprenticeship should play in this effort. Questions such as the following are considered: How can persistent and high levels of adult and youth unemployment be avoided? What are some of the likely consequences of the increase in mandatory retirement from age 65 to 70? Finally, the third dimension looks at manpower policy in the U.S. as it has been evolving since WWII and considers future directions.

Part four, "The Politics of Employment," provides for the inclusion of the political element in manpower economics, particularly in employment policy.

64. Glenn, Lowell Marshall. "Public Service Employment for the Disadvantaged." Unpublished doctoral dissertation, George Washington University, Washington, D.C., December, 1973.

This study reviews some of the alternative models for providing Public Service Employment (PSE) that have emerged or might be appropriate in the future. It explores the basic purposes to which government policies might be directed in manpower and employment activities and concludes that PSE is probably more effective as a redistribution program than as an anti-cyclical technique or a method for improving the basic employability of program participants. The study then examines the current emphasis of PSE activities and suggests that the program be redirected to better serve the needs of those who have previously been excluded from meaningful participation in the world of work.

65. Godwin, Lamond, et al. Rural Jobs from Rural Public Works: A Rural Employment Outreach Experimental and Demonstration Project, Phase One, February 1, 1976 to January 31, 1977. Washington, D.C.: The National Rural Center, 1977. NTIS PB-283 093/3GA

This report describes the activities and findings of the first year of a demonstration and experimental project designed to increase the number of local poor people hired on federally-funded construction projects in rural areas. First year's activities focused on the Tennessee-Tombigbee Waterway Project being built by the Corps of Engineer through rural areas in Alabama and Mississippi and divided into two general sections: program development and baseline data. The results of program development efforts included development and imposition of a precedent setting affirmative action plan on the Waterway project and the launching of an outreach employment program. The results of baseline data efforts stemmed from a labor market impact study of the McClellan-Kerr Arkansas River Navigation System. (NTIS)

66. Goldberg, Gertrude, et al. "Public Service Employment: A Poorly Publicized Opportunity; Title IV in the 60's." IRCD Bulletin, 8, May-September, 1972.

The first section of this issue of the Bulletin has to do with public service employment, a poorly understood social policy which must be defined before it can be evaluated as an anti-poverty strategy. The term public service employment (PSE) refers to the policy of using government funds to create jobs which serve a dual purpose: that of (1) providing paid employment for those unable to find work in the private sector of the economy, and (2) expanding vital services to people. Promising but surprisingly unnoticed legislative proposals seek to broaden, expand, or extend the Emergency Employment Act of 1971. The major criteria for evaluating PSE proposals include permanence, size, hiring preferences for the disadvantaged, community participation, and potential for upgrading. The second section is a digest of a longer report, "A Survey of Inservice Education Workshops." To understand past practices in inservice desegregation workshops, the authors examined a large body of Title IV, E.S.E.A. workshop reports. These workshop reports offer a body of knowledge about the design and effectiveness of holding small-group learning experiences to deal with the multiple and complex intellectual and human relations problems of school desegregation in an atmosphere of social change. (ERIC)

67. Goldstein, Jon H. "The Effectiveness of Manpower Training Programs: Review of Research on the Impact on the Poor," Studies in Public Welfare - Paper Number Three. Washington, D.C.: GPO, 1972. Y4.Ec7: W45/paper 19

This study was prepared by a staff member for the Joint Economic Committee's Subcommittee on Fiscal Policy. It reviews manpower training programs' impact on the earnings of the poor and assesses the likelihood that greatly expanded training programs will reduce the incidence of poverty and the size of the welfare population. (CIS)

68. Goodfellow, Gordon. Estimates of Benefits from Training. Washington, D.C.: U.S. Department of Labor, 1976. NTIS PB256331/AS

This paper presents four estimates of the effects of training on post-program earnings, wage rates, and weeks of employment for two programs--institutional training under the Manpower Development and Training Act and Job Opportunities in the Business Sector (JOBS). The first estimates were calculated from a simple pre-post comparison of the relative changes in these variables for trainees and comparison group members. The others were estimated from a regression equation using unadjusted data, adjusted data, and an interaction term. The data were drawn from 10 Standard Metropolitan Statistical Areas, two sex groups, and two race groups. The preliminary results indicated that training has a beneficial effect on trainees. However, the estimate of that effect was sensitive to choice of estimating variables, and that theory could be used to move these estimates in what is believed, a priori, to be the right direction. The observed differences between trainee and comparison group members and possible biases in trainees' observed economic behavior made it difficult to arrive at a single estimate of the effect of training. (ASPER)

69. Gramlich, Edward M. "State and Local Budgets the Day After it Rained: Why is the Surplus so High?" Brookings Papers on Economic Activity, 1, 1978, pp. 191-214.

The source of budget surpluses experienced by state and local governments in 1977 is examined in this paper. A model of state and local budgets is developed and tested with the results suggesting that much of the change experienced stems from the impact on construction expenditures as the result of some questionable properties of the Public Works Employment Act of 1976. The study also presents a comparison of hypothetical variables in the absence of the 1975 recession with such variables in a recession cushioned by either countercyclical revenue sharing or public service employment (PSE). This comparison shows (1) present programs are much smaller than what would be necessary to neutralize the effects of the recession and (2) the main impact of recession is on the tax side of state and local government budgets. Thus, expenditures appear to have been altered little by the recession, nor are they raised much by either countercyclical revenue sharing or PSE. In particular, countercyclical PSE involves displacement and unless something can be done to avoid displacement, PSE will prove disappointing as a direct stimulant to employment.

70. Greenberg, David H. "Participation in Public Employment Programs," in John L. Palmer (editor). Creating Jobs: Public Employment Programs and Wage Subsidies. Washington, D.C.: Brookings Institution, 1978, pp. 323-367.

There is little information available concerning the numbers and characteristics of persons who would participate in guaranteed employment programs if the opportunity were available. The first section of this paper considers some of the factors that determine whether individuals will decide to participate in a job creation program and suggests a methodological framework for simulating supply responses to public employment programs. After a brief discussion of the primary data source, the required parameters, and important program characteristics to be varied, a methodological framework is developed to estimate supply response to several alternative guaranteed employment programs. Finally, the paper summarizes the major results of the simulations, discusses some of the limitations of these results, and describes certain aspects of an effort to extend this research.

71. Gunderson, Morley. "Impact of Government Training Subsidies," Industrial Relations, 13, October, 1973, pp. 319-24.

Morley Gunderson's article analyzes the impact of government training subsidies by testing three hypotheses: (1) Government subsidies to on-the-job training encourages the sponsoring company to retain trainees after training (and thus there is a positive relationship between the size of the government subsidy and the probability that a beginning trainee will be retained by the sponsoring company), (2) Government subsidies to OJT encourage the sponsoring company to graduate their trainees in order to obtain the subsidy which is conditional upon the trainee's graduation (and hence a positive relationship exists between the payment of the government subsidy and the probability that a trainee will graduate from the sponsoring company's training program), (3) Once the trainee has graduated, the size of the subsidy has no effect on whether or not he will be retained by this sponsoring company (that is, no relationship exists between the size of the subsidy and the probability that a trainee will be retained, once he has graduated). The results confirm all three hypotheses. This confirmation suggests that a government subsidy induces sponsoring companies to retain their trainees only insofar as the subsidy encourages the company to graduate the trainees but does nothing to encourage the company to retain trainees once they graduate.

72. Gunderson, Morley. "Retention of Trainees: A Study with Dichotomous Dependent Variables," Journal of Econometrics, 2, May, 1974, pp. 79-93.

The purpose of this paper is to present and illustrate alternative statistical models for estimating the probability that a trainee will be retained by the sponsoring company after training and to identify the characteristics associated with such retention. The results are based on a sample of 1,240 trainees who undertook government-sponsored on-the-job training in Ontario between April 1967 and April 1969. A model incorporating a dichotomous dependent variable was tested using ordinary least squares, probit analysis and adjustments to the linear probability function made with the Oscutt, Logit and Warner transformations.A large number of explanatory variables were utilized with company and training program characteristics proving to be most important. All of the five alternative techniques provided satisfactory estimates of the probability of success.

73. Hady, Thomas F. "Will Public Service Jobs Cure Unemployment?," American Journal of Agricultural Economics, 57, December, 1975, pp. 949-52.

Public service job programs are analyzed within a framework consisting of three branches: an allocation branch, a distribution branch, and a stabilization branch. The allocation branch is concerned with the allocation of limited federal resources among competing ends. The distribution branch is concerned with the distribution of income. The stabilization branch is concerned with keeping the economy stable. The findings of this analysis are compared to a system of income guarantees assumed to be financed by the same taxes and producing the same income distribution as the proposed public employment. The author concludes that the value of public service employment is dubious. On resource allocation grounds, no clear-cut case can be made. A system of income supplements is found superior to public service employment in redistributing income with the exception of some specialized instances. On stabilization grounds, there are instances in which public service employment would have potential advantages, but a large proportion of the cases could be more effectively handled with other measures.

Therefore, the government instituted a large-scale public service employment program instead of an income supplement program based on sociopolitical arguments rather than economic rationale.

74. Hamermesh, Daniel S. Economic Aspects of Manpower Training Programs. Lexington, Massachusetts: Heath Lexington Books, 1971.

Using economic analysis to discuss possible roles and effects of government intervention in the area of manpower training is the goal of this volume. The author considers the issues of jobs for disadvantaged workers and displacement, alternative subsidies for depressed areas, the use of manpower programs to shift the Phillips Curve, and optimal mobility and other aspects of training in an urban economy. He concludes that employment and training programs should be redirected toward goals more appropriate to such intervention in private decisions, and a more efficient use of training programs in achieving those goals.

75. Hamermesh, Daniel S. "Subsidies for Jobs in the Private Sector," in John L. Palmer (editor). Creating Jobs: Public Employment Programs and Wage Subsidies. Washington, D.C.: Brookings Institution, 1978, pp. 87-122.

In this study Daniel Hamermesh analyzes many of the administrative and economic aspects of both categorical and general wage subsidies paid to employees. In the first section, various kinds of subsidies are described and both foreign and domestic examples are given. Section two discusses categorical programs of wage subsidy tried in the United States during the sixties and early seventies. The third section provides a detailed analysis of a number of economic factors essential to evaluating the impact of wage subsidies, and the next section simulates the likely impact of one such subsidy on both the amount and the distribution of employment. Finally, the overall desirability of wage subsidies is considered, and ways of increasing their likely success are recommended.

76. Hamermesh, Daniel S. and Hugh M. Pitcher. "Economic Formulas for Manpower Revenue Sharing," Industrial and Labor Relations Review, 27, July 1974, pp. 511-524.

Although revenue sharing for specific purposes has been under discussion for some time, the criteria for allocating funds have seldom been the focus of economic analysis. In an attempt to remedy that situation, this paper first develops an ideal formula to maximize the average benefit-cost ratio of projects to be undertaken by jurisdictions receiving federal funds for manpower training, and then modifies this formula to resolve problems of data availability and to include income redistribution as another goal of manpower programs. The revenue allocations implied by several variations of this formula are shown to be more favorable to large cities than the shares called for by the 1973 law initiating manpower revenue sharing, but less favorable than the allocations actually received by large cities before revenue sharing began. (ILRR)

77. Harrison, Bennett. "Public Sector Jobs and the Disadvantaged," in U.S. Congress. Emergency Employment Act of 1971, 92nd Congress, 1st Session, 1971, pp. 131-43. Y4.Ed8/1: Em 7/11

The expanding need for public services combined with the growing number of unemployed and underemployed workers makes public service employment an ideal tool for dealing with the disadvantaged. The author makes five major points to support this concept. These are: (1) the rapid growth of public sector jobs, (2) the relatively good wages paid in public service jobs, (3) the secular stability of public employment, (4) the physical access to public service jobs by the urban poor, and (5) the historical role of public employment as a "port of entry" into the world of work. Thus, the author sees public service employment as a means to alleviate the problem of the unemployed and the underemployed, in particular the working poor earning less than a poverty level of income.

78. Harrison, Bennett. "Public Service Jobs for Urban Ghetto Residents," Good Government, 86, Fall, 1969, pp. 1-20.

The case for a local public service job development program, particularly in urban ghettos, is examined. The paper begins with a study of the past, present and most likely future course of growth in the demand for public services and the derived demand for public service workers. The supply side issues particular to the urban ghetto are examined. The cost and benefits of a public service job development program are then outlined and two models-- one at the State level and one at the national level--are considered.

79. Harrison, Bennett and Paul Osterman. "Public Employment and Urban Poverty: Some New Facts and a Policy Analysis," Urban Affairs Quarterly, 9, March, 1974, pp. 303-336.

Public services are explored with respect to the creation and funding of Community Development Corporations (CDC) in urban and rural poverty areas. The authors suggest that policy makers experiment with the subcontracting of CDC's by local governments for the provision of outreach recruiting and pre-vocational training services, as well as the management of selected public service facilities located in the ghetto, particularly in the fields of public health and welfare.

The relationship between the public and private sectors is also a very important aspect. Government contracts to private industry that produce goods and services, unlikely to be produced otherwise, can contribute to employment growth. The data suggest that the public service will be the major "growth sector" of tomorrow's urban economy. Major priority for future research will have to be assigned to the analysis of public service job programming as a strategy for combatting urban poverty. (ERIC)

80. Hartz, John. Systems of Career/Occupational Information for Youth and Other CETA Participants: Guidelines and Considerations for CETA Prime Sponsors. Washington, D.C.: Employment and Training Administration, 1979. L37.8: C18

This technical assistance guide was prepared for CETA prime sponsors for the purpose of providing information on what is known about career decision-making and the delivery of career information within the context of employment and training programs. In addition, issues and considerations which should be addressed by program planners and operators in implementing programs are raised.

81. Haveman, Robert H. "The Dutch Social Employment Program," in John L. Palmer (editor). Creating Jobs: Public Employment Programs and Wage Subsidies. Washington, D.C.: Brookings Institution, 1978, pp. 241-275.

In this study, the structure and performance of the Social Employment program of the Netherlands is described and evaluated. In the first section the organization and financial structure of the Dutch Social Employment program are described and major patterns of employment and cost growth are summarized. Using a benefit-cost framework, the industrial centers component of the Dutch program is analyzed in section two. In the final section, some lessons of the Dutch experience in providing income support and employment for less productive workers are drawn and related to current U.S. policy discussions.

82. Hedlund, Ronald D. and Chava Nachmias. "The Impact of CETA on Work Orientations," in David Nachmias (editor). The Practice of Policy Evaluation. New York, New York: St. Martin's Press, 1980, pp. 80-114.

The Hedlund-Nachmias study focuses on the effect of CETA-TITLE VI employment on work-attitude changes in participants. Following a discussion of the locale (Milwaukee County, Wisconsin) and the method used to collect the data reported here, this study describes the persons who were selected as project participants and analyzes the individual and structural determinants of any attitude changes they experienced.

83. Heins, A. James. "The Negative Income Tax, Head Grants, and Public Employment Programs: A Welfare Analysis," Journal of Human Resources, 5, Summer, 1970, pp. 298-303.

This article uses traditional excess burden analysis to make comparative welfare judgments about the three general types of poverty programs noted in the title. Its central conclusions are: (1) a given welfare increase can be achieved at lower cost with head grants than with either of the other programs; (2) the relative cost of an employment program and a negative income tax which would generate a given increase in welfare depends on the preference pattern of the poor as between income and leisure; and (3) while it is clear that a work-subsidizing employment program would increase inducements for the poor to work, it is not clear that the resulting increase in value of product would be as great as the value of the subsidy required to generate its forthcoming. (JHR)

84. Hellerman, Herbert and Michael Tannen. "Optimal Manpower Planning in Local Labor Markets: A Planning Model," Quarterly Review of Economics and Business, 16, Winter, 1976, pp. 55-68.

This study presents a computer-oriented linear programming model of optimal placement of clients in manpower programs. The purpose of the model is to provide an application of economic theory which can aid local planners in determining the best placement of different population group members into available manpower programs. The authors suggest that working with the model will permit useful experiments to explore the effects of policies on client placement before the actual implementation of these policies takes place. They also point out that before the model can be utilized, the planner must possess certain information in order to obtain the set of results indicating optimal client placement. This information is presented in an outline of eight main factors to be considered in applying the model.

85. Herrnstadt, Irwin L., Morris A. Horowitz, and Marlene B. Seltzel. The Implementation of CETA in Boston, 1974-77. Boston, Massachusetts: Northeastern University, 1977. NTIS PB-270 402/1ST

A case study of the introduction of the Comprehensive Employment and Training Act (CETA) in Boston, was conducted: (1) to chronicle and analyze the changes in employment and training programs as the federal policy changes from a centralized and categorical policy to a decentralized and decategorized one; (2) to examine the impact of those changes on employment and training programs and institutions; the internal structure and staffing of these institutions; program participants and the community; and (3) to study how the CETA Prime Sponsor monitors and evaluates its programs. Open-ended interviews were conducted with strategic members of the city, state, and private institutions engaged in either planning or operating employment and training programs. Program data pertaining to client characteristics, enrollments, termination, and work experiences were collected. The eleven principal findings included these three: (1) Aside from Public Service Employment, the introduction of CETA has not changed Boston's Manpower system greatly; (2) A restructuring of the administrative system did permit incorporation of several new youth programs and it does permit special attention to the needs of ex-offenders, drug addicts, older workers, and women; and (3) Due to the weakness of the local economy and administrative defects in the program, there was a substantial cutback of on-the-job training. (ERIC)

86. Hobbie, Richard A. and Alan Fein. Public Employment and Training Assistance: Alternative Federal Approaches. Washington D.C.: Congressional Budget Office, 1977.

An analysis of the structural elements of the employment situation was undertaken in 1977 to provide congressional members with information to use in making policy decisions about the federal role and budget in employment and training programs. It is concluded that the federal government can implement four basic budget strategies: create additional jobs; increase the skills of certain types of workers; provide income assistance to workers experiencing employment problems; and reduce discriminatory practices. Although participants in Public Service Employment programs in 1976 came in high proportions from low-income and minority groups, training programs placed a greater emphasis on the disadvantaged and youth populations. Public Service Employment can increase the current earnings of unemployed workers, but it is doubtful that there are any lasting gains in future earnings. There are low annual earnings gains from training programs in relation to costs; however, training programs may find opportunities for youth, minorities, and the economically disadvantaged not available in the private sector. This booklet has a chapter describing recent trends in employment, training, and related income assistance policy; discusses the four possible policy options for 1978; and includes twenty-four tables of statistics regarding the participants costs and effects of various employment, training, and assistance programs. (ERIC)

87. Hoffman, Saul D. "On-The-Job Training: Differences by Race and Sex," _Monthly Labor Review_, 104, July, 1981, pp. 34-36.

On-the-job training is an important determinant of individual earnings and particularly the growth of earnings over time. This study found that blacks and women receive less training on-the-job than do white males and a smaller percentage of these groups are currently receiving training. Consequently, a wider earnings gap between blacks, women and white males is expected over time with a more permanent low-wage condition existing for blacks and women. The evidence on race/sex training differentials reported in this study is the result of a survey undertaken by the Panel Study of Income Dynamics.

88. Horney, N., F. Sistruk, R. Baybrook, M. S. Raich, and B. B. Ellis. _An Evaluative Study of CETA Non-Profit PSE in Florida_. Tampa, Florida: University of South Florida Press, 1980.

This monograph is an impact assessment of the PSE programs in Florida for fiscal year 1978. The study examines both short-run and long-run effects of PSE programs on participants through an analysis of archival data, and the administration of a mail survey emphasizing targeting, training, and transition to unsubsidized employment. A profile of the participants is presented, and a before-and-after comparison of the labor market experience of the participants is undertaken covering wages, occupational status, training-relatedness, job satisfaction, job tenure, and length of employment. (ERIC)

89. Horowitz, Stanley A. and George F. Brown. _The Impact of Labor Market Conditions on MDTA Completion Status_. Washington, D.C.: U.S. Department of Labor, 1974. NTIS PB 253187/AS

The model underlying the empirical work undertaken in this study sought to explain the fraction of the terminees of Manpower Development Training Act (MDTA) institutional training who end up in each of four groups (full-time completers, early completers, those who leave for jobs, and dropouts) as a function of the value of the enrollees' characteristics in the labor market and the nature of labor market opportunities available to them. Variables of the completion status, enrollee characteristics, labor market conditions, and program factors were incorporated in multiple regression analysis. It is concluded that trainees viewed the program as an alternative labor market opportunity, so that labor market conditions had a strong impact on enrollment and completion rates. Other demographic variables have an impact on the nature of enrollee termination status, while program composition factors have no notable impact. (ASPER)

90. IMPACT, Inc. Guidelines to Effecting Coordination: WIN and CETA. Washington, D.C.: Employment and Training Administration, 1978. L37.8: C78

This Technical Assistance Guide is designed to assist state and local WIN and CETA program sponsors in the process of coordinating their services. It deals with how the coordination process occurs and how critical decisions are made throughout the process, which will yield various types of program coordination. Based on inten- sive observation of a variety of coordination efforts including increased communication, shared information, referral agreements, joint clients, single inter-program reporting systems and alloca- tion of staff, several general phases and specific steps in their development and implementation were identified. These factors were determined to influence the eventual utility and longevity of the various efforts.

91. Jacobson, Louis S. The Use of Longitudinal Data to Assess the Impact of Manpower Training on Earnings. Washington, D.C.: U.S. Department of Labor, 1973. NTIS PB253579/AS

This study reviews research using Social Security data to measure the effect of government training programs on the earnings of participants. Social Security's Continuous Work History Sample (CWHS) was used to demonstrate that prior studies have substan- tially underestimated the impact of training on earnings. Those studies employed a model of income determination that did not take account of trainees, being induced to join the program because of difficulty in finding or holding adequate jobs. The basic technique used in this study is a comparison of actual post-training earnings of trainees with the earnings of a control group whose earnings potential at the time of initiation of training was identical to that of the participants. To compare the two groups, a model of income determination is specified and estimated using regression analysis. Because it was not possible to identify trainees in the CWHS or to obtain a reliable measure of unemployment and loss of job tenure in the summary earnings records, the estimation proce- dure is based on knowledge of the simple correlations among the variables. (ASPER)

92. Jamroz, Deborah. "Public Service Employment: Its Role in a Changing Economy," Federal Reserve Bank of New York Quarterly, 4, Spring, 1979, pp. 34-38.

Deborah Jamroz analyzes the effectiveness of CETA in combating cyclical and structural unemployment. Initially, CETA was organ- ized into four separate programs each with its own specific objec- tives. Originally, Title II was the principal job-creation program, but in December of 1974, due to rising unemployment, a temporary countercyclical program, Title VI, was added. With Title VI addressing the cyclical unemployment problem, Title II became specifically directed towards the low-income and long-term unemployed. The author concludes that programs such as Title VI are successful in providing temporary jobs and income support to workers during recessionary periods. Since public employment can be implemented relatively quickly and is likely to create more jobs per dollar spent than other policies, it is an effective short-run countercyclical tool. However, its effectiveness declines over time as local agencies come to rely increasingly on Federal funds. Public service programs can also be effective in reducing structural unemployment if the composition of local employment is altered to include those workers who are disadvantaged, and if these workers are trained in jobs that will allow them to transition to private sector employment.

93. Job, Barbara C. "More Public Services Spur Growth in Government Employment," Monthly Labor Review, 101, September, 1978, pp. 3-7.

This study analyzes the growth in local, state and federal governments from 1957 through 1977. Employment at the state and local level has forged ahead at a brisk pace, increasing at an annual average rate of 4.3 percent since 1957. Of the 29 million jobs created in the past two decades, 1 in 4 was in state and local government. During this same period, federal government employment grew less dramatically at an annual average rate of 1 percent. The growth in employment at all levels took place primarily as a result of population growth and a shift to a service orientated economy. In the future, state and local governments are expected to remain the fastest growing employment sector and changes in federal employment will be small from year to year subject to new legislation mandating new functions of government.

94. Johnson, Deborah and Collette Moser (editors). Essays on the Public Employment Program in Rural Areas. East Lansing, Michigan: Michigan State University Press, 1973.

These eight essays on the Public Employment Program (PEP) were written by members of the Rural Manpower Policy Research Consortium. Essays are titled as follows: (1) "Public Service Employment and Manpower Policies in Rural Areas, Limitations of the Emergency Employment Act--EEA," argument for integration of PEP with manpower, educational, and regional development policies; (2) "PEP-- Special Problems of Rural Areas," criticism of PEP's suitability to rural areas with a program proposal; (3) "Expansion of Needed Public Service in Rural Areas with Special Reference to the South," contrast of EEA and Operation Mainstream; (5) "PEP Needs in the Rural South," discussion of poverty, implicit and explicit barriers to public employment and analyzation of employment needs; (6) "EEA--Some Basic Policy Questions with Special Reference to American Indian Reservations," four policy considerations; (7) "Experience of the EEA in Balance-of-State Michigan; Some Implications for Revenue Sharing in Rural Areas," comparison of EEA and Revenue Sharing programs; (8) "A Comparative Study of Public Service Employment in Rural California: A Proposal," research proposal on PEP in Balance-of-State California towns. (ERIC)

95. Johnson, George E.   Evaluating the Impact of CETA Programs on Participants' Earnings: Methodological Issues and Problems. Washington, D.C.: U.S. Department of Labor, 1975. NTIS PB290389/AS

This paper reviews the conceptual issues associated with evaluating the impact of programs under the Comprehensive Employment and Training Act (CETA) of 1973. It explains the concept of net impact, stresses the use of comparison group methodology, and discusses difficulties associated with the identification of the program's net impact. A strategy for estimating relative program impact is also presented. The problem of duration of program effects--an issue that has further implications about the scale of the evaluation effort necessary to determine the efficacy of CETA--is considered. Additional conceptual difficulties in the interpretation of results, apart from the statistical problems and the question of the optimal scale of evaluation effort under CETA, are also discussed. (ASPER)

96. Johnson, George E.   The Labor Market Displacement Effect in the Analyses of the Net Impact of Manpower Programs. Washington, D.C.: U.S. Department of Labor, 1976. NTIS PB256259/AS

This study examined the meaning of new estimates of the benefits and costs of employment and training programs, concentrating on the displacement problem. The basic assumption was that if a trainee displaces an incumbent in the labor market, the trainee's gain in earnings following training overstates the benefits of the program and that, conversely, when the trainee is drawn from a weak labor market, the loss of earnings while training does not necessarily represent a loss of output because the trainee's former job is filled by another worker. The study employed a series of simple models of labor market behavior which considered: (1) Conditions of continuous full employment; (2) drawing trainees from a labor market characterized by substantial unemployment; (3) the relation between the social returns to the program and the returns that would be inferred from microeconomic data, with allowance for job turnover, particularly in short-duration jobs; and (4) substantial unemployment in the source market but continuous full employment in the receiving market, which depresses all conventional measures of social returns because the average earnings of the control group exceed the loss of output caused by removing the trainee from the source market.

Under the most likely values, social returns would exceed private returns, so that less training than desirable would occur in the absence of government programs, the study concluded. Further, for programs like the Work Incentive (WIN) Program, which attempt to move individuals from out of the labor force into low-wage employment, the analysis suggested that observed earnings increases were likely to overstate the true increase in aggregate output due to the program. For training which moves individuals from one slack market to another, the relation between observed and true social returns was not clear. (ASPER)

97. Johnson, George E. "Structural Unemployment Consequences of Job Creation Policies," in John Palmer (editor). Creating Jobs: Public

Employment Programs Wage Subsidies.   Washington, D.C.:   Brookings
Institution, 1978, pp. 123-152.

In this study George Johnson concentrates on selected issues
associated with programs aimed at improving the labor market
position of the disadvantaged. The first section investigates the
impact on output, employment and the distribution of net income due
to an economy-wide subsidy and unskilled labor. Section two
examines problems associated with the use of the public sector as
the exclusive vehicle for subsidizing low-wage labor.

98. Johnson, George E. and Gary Reed.   The Evaluation of the WIN II
Program: Methodological Issues and Some Initial Results. Washington,
D.C.: U.S. Department of Labor, 1974. NTIS PB283673/AS

This paper examines the major problems in conducting an impact
evaluation of the Work Incentive (WIN) Program as modified by the
Talmadge Amendments of 1971 (WIN II). The inability to develop a
set of precise estimates of the benefits directly attributable to
the program is stressed. This limitation of the study is due to
the nonavailability of adequate evaluation data. Some tentative
conclusions are drawn about the impact of the program and the
possibilities of drawing more definitive conclusions. The principal
conclusions are as follows: (1) Estimates of both the increase in
earnings due to participation during the first year and the rate at
which this net impact depreciates over time are needed to assess
the net impact of WIN II and of welfare savings. (2) Deterrent
effects can be detected only through the use of aggregate data. (3)
The WIN II program is likely to have different effects on the well-
being of different socioeconomic groups. (4) A primary benefit of
the WIN II program is on future generations. (5) Although incon-
clusive, evidence on the impact of WIN I would be relevant for
assessing the impact of WIN II. (6) Using indirect evidence on
completer job entry rates, wages for completer job entries, and
previous information on welfare turnover rates, range estimates of
increased earnings and welfare savings due to participation in WIN
II can be calculated. (7) The estimates of the social rate of
return to resources allocated to the WIN program range from zero to
a ridiculously high number. (8) The range estimates of welfare
savings attributable to WIN II vary as much as the range estimates
of increases in net earnings. (9) A cursory examination of the
behavior of aggregate AFDC costs over time might indicate that WIN
II has a substantial impact on lowering welfare costs. (10)
Analysis of inter-State data on welfare costs suggests that WIN
placement reduces AFDC costs by about 30 percent of the monthly
costs of a single AFDC family. (ASPER)

99. Johnson, George E. and Gary Reed.   Further Evidence on the Impact
of the WIN II Program. Washington, D.C.: U.S. Department of Labor,
1975. NTIS PB 283558/AS

This paper extended and refines the range estimates of the net
impact of WIN II on participants earnings that were derived in an
earlier study entitled "The Evaluation of the WIN II Program:
Methodological Issues and Some Initial Results." The methodology,
adopted from the earlier study, is used to infer estimates of WIN

II impact on participant earnings from indirect evidence, including regular program data, revised estimates of WIN II job placements, and data on the movement of AFDC recipients in and out of employment. This study utilizes more detailed data and extends the range estimates into fiscal year 1974, but the methodology used suffers from the same weaknesses present in the earlier study. The estimates presented are too imprecise to be considered as reliable estimates of net program impact and should be viewed as partially-informed guesses. The rough estimates presented suggest that the rapid increase in WIN II placements during fiscal years 1973-74 represent, to a large extent, normal flows of welfare recipients into employment that would have occurred in the absence of the program. It is clearly demonstrated that the rapid increase in gross job placements resulting from the transition of WIN from a training (WIN I) to a direct placement (WIN II) program is consistent with a small net program impact on participants' employment and earnings. (ASPER)

100. Johnson, George E. and James D. Tomola. The Efficacy of Public Service Employment Programs. Washington, D.C.: U.S. Department of Labor, 1975. NTIS PB257267/AS

This study addressed five major evaluation questions associated with Public Service Employment (PSE).

It concluded that there is a severe potential problem of a fiscal substitution effect, i.e., State and local governments may use PSE subsidies to do what they would have done anyway and simply reduce property and other local taxes. Although most Public Employment Program (PEP) participants appeared to be from the middle of the skill distribution, data on all State and local government hiring during the period were not available. A major advantage of the PSE approach was that it gets more people to work more quickly than other forms of fiscal policy, and the analysis of the short-run effects of PSE on aggregate employment confirmed this. Estimates of the inflationary impact of a large-scale PSE program (without fiscal substitution) were presented. Unless PSE programs concentrate on workers of higher than average skill level, they will be no more inflationary than other forms of fiscal policy per unit of unemployment reduction.

There was no reliable evidence on which to draw concerning two other important evaluation questions: The degree to which participation in PSE augments human capital and the degree to which PSE participants were used effectively. (ASPER)

101. Johnson, George E. and James D. Tomola. Fiscal Substitution Effect of Alternative Approaches to Public Service Employment Policy. Washington, D.C.: U.S. Department of Labor, 1976. NTIS PB281452/AS

This paper examines the question of the size and importance of the fiscal substitution effect of Public Service Employment (PSE) programs. A conceptual model for the determination of the level of State and local employment is developed, and the implications of three variants of PSE programs (wage subsidies, federalized programs, and lump sum grants with maintenance of effort restrictions) are explored. The model is applied to aggregate time series data in an effort to estimate the relevant parameters (including the fiscal substitution effect of current PSE programs for an evaluation of the relative efficacy of the alternative approaches) for increasing State and local employment. The conceptual interdependence of the fiscal substitution effect and the impact of PSE on the composition of State and local employment by "quality" is also explored.

It is concluded that: (1) The importance of the size of the fiscal substitution effect in assessing the efficacy of PSE depends on the objectives of the program. (2) There are several ways in which PSE programs can be set up and four alternatives are examined from a theoretical point of view with respect to their employment creation potential. (3) Empirical analyses suggest that the fiscal substitution effect of PSE is very small for two or three quarters after introduction into a PSE slot but then rises to about 100 percent after five quarters, and that the traditional PSE format, as represented by PEP and CETA, is probably more effective than a wage subsidy in increasing State and local employment up to a year after triggering the program but thereafter the reverse is true. (4) An analysis of the effect of PSE on the skill composition of employment demand suggests that although PSE participants are much less employable in a long-run sense than the average State and local employee, they are not much different in this respect than the average member of the labor force. This conclusion, however, must be qualified by the possibility that fiscal substitution is skill specific (i.e., local governments hire their low-skilled non-PSE work forces at their pre-PSE levels). (ASPER)

102. Johnson, George E. and James D. Tomola. "The Fiscal Substitution Effect of Alternative Approaches to Public Service Employment Policy," Journal of Human Resources, 12, Winter 1977, pp. 3-26.

The size of the fiscal substitution effect is important in evaluating public service employment as either a counter-cyclical policy or as revenue-sharing. Empirically, the effect appears to be very small for one or two quarters, but rises to about 100 percent after five quarters. From an anti-poverty perspective, however, composition effects are most important. Although PSE program employees appear representative of the total labor force, the proportion of the disadvantaged among PSE participants is greater than the proportion of them in state and local government employment. (JHR)

103. Johnson, Miriam and Marged Sugarman. Job Development and Placement: CETA Program Models. Washington, D.C.: Employment and Training Administration, 1978. L37.816: J57

This study is concerned with those job development and placement functions in employability development programs which result in direct, indirect, and self-directed placements into unsubsidized employment. It traces the historical development of the placement function and draws lessons for current practitioners from the mistakes and successes of the past. It develops a model of job recruiting and job search and suggests strategies which might be

useful to program planners. Recommendations stress raising the
quality of CETA placements, infusing a more professional approach
into the placement functions and developing the self-help capabilities of clients.

104. Jones, E. Terrence and Donald Phares. "CETA Billions Distributed
Randomly," Nation's Cities, 16, July, 1978, pp. 14-17.

Authors E. Terrence Jones and Donald Phares shed light on the
faults of the formula funding process being used by the Federal
government to distribute billions of dollars in CETA grants. The
problem is derived from the lack of fit between the demands of the
formula and the statistical resources that are being used. This
discrepancy causes conflict in that the statistical resources are
unable to support the policy intent of CETA. The core of the CETA
formula is unemployment. The unemployment rate that enters the
formula is obtained from two "official" sources, The Current
Population Survey (CPS) and each individual state's division of
employment security. A third unemployment rate used in this
analysis is derived from a statistical survey done by a team of
researchers directed by the author. It employed a methodology that
is identical to that of the Bureau of the Census but relies on more
updated information to more accurately portray local conditions.
There are startling differences between the three unemployment
rates. Several errors relate to the Census Bureau's estimates.
Another source of error is the likelihood that the completion rate
for the census survey in central cities is not as high as statistical criteria would mandate. Yet another source of error is the
Census's dependence on information contained in the most recent
decennial census. Although it is not possible to precisely calcu-
late the underestimation, it is estimated that the city of St.
Louis lost about $2 million per year in CETA revenues for each
percentage point the unemployment rate is understated.

105. Jones, E. Terrence and Donald Phares. "Formula Feedback and
Central Cities: The Case of the Comprehensive Employment and Training
Act," Urban Affairs Quarterly, 14, September, 1978, pp. 31-54.

This study critically examines the measurement of the Comprehensive
Employment and Training Act's key allocation variable unemployment.
The analysis indicates that: (1) actual unemployment rates during
the study period (September-November 1975) in the research site
(City of St. Louis), as measured by three independently conducted
surveys, are much higher than the official government estimates;
and (2) the methods used by the U.S. Bureau of the Census and the
U.S. Bureau of Labor Statistics to measure state and local
unemployment have several weaknesses, some of which apparently lead
to an underestimation of unemployment in older central cities.
(UAQ)

106. Katz, Harry and Michael Wiseman. "An Essay on Subsidized Employ-
ment in the Public Sector," in Job Creation Through Public Service
Employment, Volume 3. Washington D.C.: National Commission for
Manpower Policy, 1978. Y3.M31: 1/6/V.3

This paper discusses Subsidized Employment in the Public Sector (SEPS) which is comprised of four identifiable SEPS programs: the Public Employment Program (PEP) funded by the Emergency Employment Act of 1971, the jobs created by Title II of CETA of 1973, the countercyclical public employment initiated as part of CETA by the Emergency Jobs and Unemployment Assistance Act of 1974, and employment generated under the Emergency Job Programs Extension Act of 1976.   The paper is divided into seven sections in which SEPS programs are outlined, interpreted and major problem areas of implementation are discussed.   The authors conclude that difficulties in operating current SEPS programs have been traced to the often interrelated problems of conflicting and poorly specified objectives, lack of output measures, uncertainty concerning cost of production and unenforceable contracts.

The authors reason that the problem of implementation and operation of a grants-in-aid policy would not be easily solved by any type of comprehensive reform or a new round of regulation writings.   A discussion of the CETA extension proposal draft released by the Department of Labor on January 28, 1978, was made covering five significant features of the proposal that affect SEPS.   The authors conclude that the changes in the SEPS program incorporated in the CETA extension proposal would modestly improve the impact of the program on the incomes and unemployment of disadvantaged workers. Improvements in this direction are weakened by the failure of the proposal to clarify the programs objectives to provide prime sponsors with the opportunity to create jobs suitable for a structural SEPS program or to alter the basic SEPS contract.

107. Keller, Judy, et al. Employment and Training Programs. Washington, D.C.: Federal Programs Information and Assistance Project, 1979.

Federal training and employment resources for developmentally disabled persons are described in this volume.   The first section provides a brief historical background of the Federal Government's involvement in employment and training, beginning with the 1930's up to the passage of Section 504 of the Rehabilitation Act of 1973. Section II examines seven components of CETA: (1) administrative provisions;   (2) comprehensive employment and training services; (3) special federal responsibilities;   (4) youth programs;   (5) countercyclical Public Service Employment;   (6) private sector opportunities;   and (7) young adult conservation corps.   Considered in separate sections are the following employment and training programs: (1) The Apprenticeship Training Program;   (2) Federal Employment Work Incentive programs;   (3) Title XX Funding programs; (4) Small Business Administration Handicapped Assistance Loans;   (5) University Affiliated Facilities;   and (6) miscellaneous programs such as innovation and expansion grants.   Among eleven appendices are a list of CETA State Employment and Training Councils, and Title XX State agencies.   (ERIC)

108. Kemper, Peter and Philip Moss.   "Economic Efficiency of Public Employment Programs," in John Palmer (editor). Creating Jobs: Public Employment Programs and Wage Subsidies.   Washington, D.C.:   Brookings Institution, 1978, pp. 277-322.

The Kemper-Moss study presents a framework for evaluating the efficiency of public employment programs and examining potential trade-offs among their multiple goals. The analysis is based on insights gained from examining the early experience of a public service employment program called Supported Work, which began as a national demonstration in 1975. After a brief description of the national Supported Work demonstration, the tasks involved in creating jobs and the criteria used for evaluating the demonstration are discussed. The heart of the analysis of the efficiency trade-offs follows. Finally, there is a summary of implications of the analysis.

109. Kesselman, Jonathan R. "Work Relief Programs in the Great Depression," in John L. Palmer (editor). Creating Jobs: Public Employment Programs and Wage Subsidies. Washington, D.C.: Brookings Institution, 1978, pp. 153-240.

The author organizes the insights of 1930's work relief observers within a modern macroeconomic framework. The early views are examined and extended using later developments in economic analysis. Administrative and political factors affecting the work relief production process, material and capital inputs, workers eligibility, compensation, and program financing have logical places in the structure of a macro model. The author concludes by applying the insights from 1930's work relief to the design of modern-day employment policies.

110. Ketron, Inc. Documentation for the Public Use Data Base for the Evaluation of the Long Term Impacts of the Work Incentive Program (WIN II). Washington, D. C.: Ketron, Inc., 1979.

This three volume set provides the documentation for the longitudinal evaluation of WIN II reported by Ketron in The Long Term Impacts of WIN II. (#111) Volume I provides a description of the data base, Volume II presents a detailed description of each data element, and Volume III exhibits the data collection instruments.

111. Ketron, Inc. The Long Term Impact of WIN II: A Longitudinal Evaluation of the Employment Experiences of Participants in the Work Incentive Program. Final Report. Washington, D.C.: Ketron, Inc., 1980.

This report is the outcome of a major research effort aimed at evaluating the longitudinal impacts of the WIN II program. It follows the 1976 report on the Impact of WIN II by Pacific Consultants, Camil Associates and Ketron and is based on four waves of longitudinal interviews with over 4,300 participants and produces a three-year post-program follow-up which estimates, tracks and projects into the future program impacts. Net impacts of the program were found to include: (1) lifetime earnings benefits of $494 for males and $1,318 for females with about 91 percent of the first-year benefits disappearing in the second year following WIN, (2) modest impacts on welfare grant reduction, and (3) a bias in favor of those with higher education levels. Differential WIN impacts include: (1) women benefiting considerably from work experience and vocational training, (2) both men and women benefiting from on-the-job training with total benefits estimated for men of $7,226 and for women of $5,130, (3) public service employment providing strong earnings gains for both males and females with females gaining the most, and (4) job placement assistance provided without any other WIN training or employment component, doing little to increase earnings.

112. Kiefer, Nicholas M.   The Economic Benefits from Manpower Training Programs.   Washington, D.C.:   U.S. Department of Labor, 1976.   NTIS PB265949/AS

> This study analyzed the effect of training on earnings of trainees in four programs: (1) Manpower Development and Training Act-- Institutional Program (MDTA); (2) Job Opportunities in the Business Sector (JOBS); Job Corps (JC); and (4) Neighborhood Youth Corps (NYC/OS). The Office of Economic Opportunity/Department of Labor longitudinal data set which has been linked with annual earnings records from the Social Security Administration was used in the analysis.   Comparisons of trainee and comparison group earnings during the period surrounding training were adjusted for different distributions of age, education, and marital status between groups. Effects of training on earnings were found to vary considerably by program, sex, and race.   The adult training programs, MDTA and JOBS, greatly increased the earnings of female trainees.   The effect of training on the earnings of adult males was less clear. The two youth programs had even less precisely measured effects than the adult programs.   An estimate of the impact of training on earnings over the life cycle was recommended for analysis of the long-term benefits from the programs.   (ASPER)

113. Kiefer, Nicholas M.   Econometric Analysis of the Effect of Training Under MDTA.   Washington, D.C.:   U.S. Department of Labor, 1978.   NTIS PB290324/AS

> This paper develops econometric techniques for studying training programs using longitudinal data.   These techniques are applied to analyze the effect of Manpower Development and Training Act (MDTA) classroom training on the employment and earnings of male trainees.

> Two separate econometric techniques are developed.   The first treats employment and earnings separately (but simultaenously) and is primarily an instrumental variable technique.   The second treats employment and earnings together by examining only the earnings of the employed, but provides more control for possible bias due to "fixed effects."

> The data are from the Office of Economic Opportunity/Department of Labor longitudinal data set and concern training that took place in 1969.   Longitudinal data on trainees and members of a comparison group are analyzed.   The analysis concludes that participation in the training programs studied had zero or small positive effect on earnings.   It is also found, in accordance with previous studies, that cross-section analyses of the effect of training can give mis- leading results and analyses based on longitudinal data are prefer- able. (ASPER)

114. Kiefer, Nicholas M.   "Federally Subsidized Occupational Training and the Employment and Earnings of Male Trainees," Journal of Econometrics, 8, August, 1978, pp. 111-125.

The impact of MDTA training on the earnings and employment probabilities of male trainees is studied on the basis of a longitudinal data set on trainees and non-trainees.   Econometric techniques which eliminate many of the ambiguities in interpreting previous estimates are used to determine that the program had little or no effect on employment or earnings of trainees in the late sixties. The author suggests that the program would be better interpreted as a pure income maintenance program rather than a subsidized skill acquisition program.

115. Kiefer, Nicholas M.   "Population Heterogeneity and Inference from Panel Data on the Effects of Vocational Education," Journal of Political Economy, 87, October, 1979, pp. 213-226.

This paper considers a model of earnings over time which incorporates individual effects and time effects without assuming that these effects are orthogonal to the variable of primary interest. The central coefficient is the effect of participation in a Manpower Development and Training Act training program on the earnings of trainees.   Since the training status of (some) individuals in the sample changes during the period of the sample, both pre- and post-training contrasts and trainee/nontrainee contrasts in earnings can be made.   An estimate of the cross-section bias in a training coefficient can be made directly.   The extent of the analogies bias in the education coefficient in regression studies is a point of current debate.   The cross-section bias in the sample analyzed is large, and the estimated effect of training is small and positive.

116. Killingsworth, Charles C.   "Manpower Evaluations: Vulnerable But Useful," Monthly Labor Review, 98, April, 1975, pp. 48-51.

An excerpt from the paper "CETA and Manpower Program Evaluation" presented to the Annual Meeting of the Industrial Relations Research Association (IRRA) December 1974, this article provides an analysis of the basis for the negative conclusions drawn from previous manpower program evaluations.   Though a number of studies have concluded that the "investments" were worthwhile, even in strictly pecuniary terms, the findings have been challenged by economists who are convinced that such programs are severly ineffective and a waste of public funds.   The primary basis of these negative conclusions is a function of uncertainties and alleged uncertainties, i.e., since manpower studies fail to provide absolutely certain proof of training benefits, the benefits must be nonexistent.   Killingsworth suggests that we should ask whether the evaluation studies of manpower training establish a "reasonable probability" that the programs are worth what they cost.

The author also considers the argument that public service employment may have only a very small long-run effect on employment as a result of displacement.   Killingsworth poses three points to consider: (1) that this argument is based entirely on speculation rather than direct evidence; (2) to the extent that displacement does occur, the secondary effects will at least partially offset the displacement; and (3) if experience does show a real problem here, there is a simple and effective remedy: let the federal government administer the public service employment program.

117. Kolberg, William H. Developing Manpower Legislation: A Personal Chronicle. Washington, D.C.: National Academy of Sciences, 1978.

This work reflects a study of the development and passage of employment legislation between 1973 and 1977 with its primary focus on how the Comprehensive Employment and Training Act (CETA) became law. The author is a former Assistant Secretary of Labor and administrator of the Employment and Training Administration (1973-1977). The first of four chapters traces Congress and the Administration's four years of conflict over manpower reform. The conflict culminates in President Nixon's signing of the 1973 CETA Bill. Three results of the 1973 CETA legislation are identified: (1) major decentralization was accomplished and a strong federal role was preserved; (2) Title I authorized a decategorized program, Title III added categories for Indians and migrants, and retained an emphasis on youth, and Title IV continued the Job Corps; and (3) a separate identifiable program for Public Service Employment was included in a comprehensive bill. Chapter two discusses the effects of the 1974 oil embargo on unemployment. The corresponding period of inflation and recession, and the resulting emergency legislation are examined. Chapter three reports on the 1974 passage of the Unemployment Insurance Program, while the final chapter reviews the events which led to the assignment of Title II monies to the Title VI Public Service Employment (PSE) program. (ERIC)

118. Lawrence, Frederick T. et al. Transportation as a Factor in the Delivery of Rural Manpower Services in Public Service Employment. Montpelier, Vermont: Vermont State Employment Service, 1973. NTIS TB 232 177/6GI

The Vermont experimental and demonstration Manpower Pilot project placed low income, unemployed individuals in wage subsidized job slots in public and nonprofit agencies, anticipating that the work experience and related job skills gained would enable them to acquire nonsubsidized employment. A quantitative analysis is presented of 196 special work clients, confronted with the problems of private transportation. Although sincere efforts were made to combat each individual transportation problem, (training-related expense monies for repairs, car pools, etc.), it was found that the severe lack of public transportation and poor condition of private vehicles were, in many cases, the prime factors for clients terminating training. Several suggested solutions are presented. (ERIC)

119. Lehne, R. "Revenue Sources and Local Government Employment," Public Finance Quarterly. 3, October, 1975, pp. 400-410.

This note explores the relationship between variations in local government employment patterns and grant-in-aid receipts for three time periods, 1957-62, 1962-67, and 1967-72. Three dimensions of local government employment patterns are explored: per capita payroll cost, average monthly wage per employee, and the number of public employees per capita. The methodology follows the "determinants" analysis of public expenditure levels. The relationship between revenue sources and local government employment practices assumes different forms in different time periods.

120. Lekachman, Robert. Public Service Employment Jobs for All. Public Affairs Pamphlet No. 481. New York, New York: Public Affairs Committee, Inc., 1972.

An argument for public service jobs as a means of ameliorating structural unemployment is presented. The author argues that a program such as that suggested by the National Commission on Technology, Automation and Economic Progress could be instituted. It would create five million permanent public sector jobs and would not be inflationary if it were funded by taxes on savings and property accumulation and accompanied by cutbacks where expenditures create few jobs--oil interest, subsidies to military, large farms, etc. Because we are moving towards a "services" rather than a "goods" oriented economy, a program such as this would provide additional services as well as aid the unemployed, according to the author.

121. Levitan, Sar A. and Garth L. Mangum (editors). CETA Training: A National Review and Eleven Case Studies. Kalamazoo, Michigan: W. E. Upjohn Institute for Employment Research, 1981.

This study focuses on the quality and effectiveness of occupational skill training being offered to adults under CETA. It examines the institutional setting within which the training took place, its content and administrative structure. It contains two major parts: a national review of CETA training and eleven case studies representing various geographic, political and demographic situations. The national review, written by Robert Taggart, synthesizes the substantial body of evidence on employment and training programs. This evidence convincingly documents the positive impacts of training in increasing future employment and earnings of participants and in providing society a positive return in its investment. According to the national study, every dollar spent on OJT returns $2.18 in social benefits according to benefit-cost estimates, while the payoff for each dollar invested in local classroom training is $1.14. In the second post-program year, the institutional training impacts are even more substantial. Longer duration training pays off. The earnings gains for classroom trainees participating over 40 weeks are nearly six times those of 11 to 20 week trainees. Immediate placement is a key factor in determining gains from classroom training.

New evidence concerning the post-program earnings for 1977 Job Corps participants and FY1976 local participants relative to control groups show that classroom trainees earned $350 more in the year after learning than a comparison group, an increase of 10 percent in annual earnings. On-the-job trainees gained $850, an 18% increase. These gains are in contrast to the patterns for fiscal 1976 work experience participants who, at best, broke even relative to like nonparticipants.

Female participants, persons with low or no earnings before entry, and middle-aged participants did particularly well in classroom training. All groups gained more from OJT than work experience, and all but minority females gained more from classroom training than work experience.

The ends and means of the CETA system or its success should be reoriented in light of future prospects and the evidence that long-term training pays off most. Training and the development of human capital rather than job creation should receive priority. Where jobs are provided, they should be combined with and lead into training. Placement must be emphasized, particularly for long duration training. Mechanisms are needed to facilitate mobility from high unemployment and poverty areas.

The purpose of the case studies was to gain insight into the CETA system to determine how the varied local decisions and developments produce these aggregate results and to assess the same reality from the delivery perspective.

The eleven prime sponsors include three moderate-sized cities (Worcester, Seattle and Tucson); four large cities (Baltimore, Dallas, Indianapolis and San Francisco, each with a populace of over 500,000); one metropolitan county (Montgomery) and a consortium of three rural counties (Penolscot); a state acting as a single prime sponsor (Utah); and a balance-of-state (North Carolina).

122. Levitan, Sar A. and Garth L. Mangum. Federal Training and Work Programs in the Sixties. Ann Arbor, Michigan: Institute of Labor and Industrial Relations, 1969.

The volume discusses the development of employment and training programs aimed at disadvantaged workers. The major programs funded by the federal government are discussed in detail. These include the Manpower Development and Training Act (MDTA), Vocational Education, Job Corps, Neighborhood Youth Corps, Work Experience and Training, Vocational Rehabilitation, and the Federal-State Employment Service. The work concludes with an analysis of the status of such programs and makes recommendations for future coordination and consolidation efforts.

123. Levitan, Sar A. and Garth L. Mangum (editors). The T in CETA: Local and National Perspectives. Kalamazoo, Michigan: W. E. Upjohn Institute for Employment Research, 1981.

The focus of this study is the quality, effectiveness and management of CETA occupational skill training and CETA complements to employability development such as basic education, English as a foreign language, and training for job search. The study emphasizes the role of these factors in locally operated adult skill programs and attempts not only to assess CETA training, but also to describe its content, institutional setting and administrative structure.

This volume consists of three major parts: a summary of findings and recommendations, a review of the evidence from a national perspective and summaries of eleven case studies. The complete case studies are published in the companion volume CETA Training: A National Review and Eleven Case Studies by the same authors. From the evidence, the authors made the following conclusions:

(1) CETA training is a sound social investment; the social returns for each dollar spent on CETA-funded classroom training amounted to $1.14, while each dollar spent in OJT returned $2.28.

(2) The quality of classroom training is primarily a product of the local institutions. The prime sponsors depend on the performance of: (a) education and training institutions; (b) the public employment service; and (c) local community-based organizations.

(3) Persistent obstacles to CETA's improvements include: (a) the federal prime sponsor rating system which credits procedure rather than substance and neither measures nor rewards quality; (b) the data system which measures short-run rather than long-run outcomes; (c) the high payoff of OJT which is also not apparent to the prime sponsor in the short-run; and (d) the federal budgetary process which denies prime sponsors the opportunity for long-range planning.

(4) Training and employability development should be made the highest priority of the CETA system.

(5) To induce employers to provide on-the-job training, subsidies should cover a "try-out" period during which the trainee is in the workplace but receiving a CETA stipend until the employer has an opportunity to assess the trainee's worth.

124. Levitan, Sar A. and Robert Taggart (editors). Emergency Employment Act: The PEP Generation. Salt Lake City, Utah: Olympus Press, 1974.

This volume provides summaries of the experience with the Public Employment Program (PEP) under the Emergency Employment Act of 1971. The program was designed as a "pilot" program to make jobs available through the public sector at a time of high unemployment. The summaries generally conclude that the PEP experience did not generally do much to impact local or aggregate unemployment rates, the jobs provided were as "real" as any other state or local employment, those hired were predominantly Vietnam veterans, the program experienced limited success with transition into more permanent positions, and the decentralization of decision-making authority created problems at the beginning. Yet, PEP did demonstrate that a public employment program can be an effective counter-cyclical tool if the scale is appropriate and we learn from the PEP experience.

125. Levitan, Sar A. and Robert Taggart. "The Emergency Employment Act: An Interim Assessment," Monthly Labor Review, 95, June, 1972, pp. 3-11.

In this report Levitan and Taggart assess the progress of the Emergency Employment Act of 1971. The authors critique several aspects of the program such as objectives, implementation, decentralization, job choice, and participants. This evaluation relies heavily on case studies of state and local experience, combined with analysis of legislative and administrative developments at the national level.

126. Levitan, Sar A. and Robert Taggart. Evaluation of the First 18 Months of the Public Employment Program. Washington, D.C.: GPO, 1973.

This report evaluates the first 18 months of the Public Employment Program (PEP). PEP was the first large-scale public employment effort since the New Deal. During fiscal 1972 and 1973, the federal government provided $1.6 billion for the hiring of the unemployed. Despite its healthy pricetag, PEP was limited in its impact. The PEP funds met only a fraction of the needs faced by state and local governments. It was estimated that there were 25 unemployed for every slot. However, the author points out that PEP was not a failure. Although insufficient, PEP jobs had an impact on unemployment, delivered needed services, helped specific target groups, and provided transitional opportunities to minority participants. The hurried implementation of PEP, the variability from area to area, as well as the abrupt deceleration of the program, made overall assessment of PEP (after 18 months) difficult. Successes and failures on each front must be weighed in light of the necessary trade-offs. It must be determined whether more could have been accomplished in one area without sacrificing elsewhere, whether the compromise achieved was appropriate, given existing conditions and financial constraints, and whether a different combination of goals should be sought in the future.

127. Levitan, Sar A. and Gregory Wurzburg. Evaluating Federal Social Programs - An Uncertain Art. Kalamazoo, Michigan: W. E. Upjohn Institute for Employment Research, 1979.

This study examines the tools that social program evaluators have developed and reviews the institutional arrangements that have been devised for the care and nourishment of the evaluators. It assesses the comparative strengths and weaknesses of the evaluation establishments in two particular branches of government—the executive and legislative—and concentrates on programs assigned to the Department of Labor and Department of Health, Education and Welfare. These are the two federal agencies with primary responsibility for administering social programs as well as the principal sources of insights for policy making in both branches. The authors recognize the need for evaluation of social programs and for the use of the best available evaluation methodologies. However, they detail serious limitations of both evaluation tools and institutional arrangements for federal program evaluation. They question whether the tools available to evaluators and the climate in which they work permit them to design either objective criteria or valid and reliable methods. In conclusion, the authors suggest that the central issue for scrutiny is whether evaluation as it is practiced provides a convincing basis for making decisions about social programs.

128. Levitan, Sar A. and Joyce K. Zickler. The Quest for a Federal Manpower Partnership. Cambridge, Massachusetts: Harvard University Press, 1974.

This study reviews the development of manpower program administration and planning during the nearly twelve years that elapsed between the passage of the Manpower Development and Training Act and the Comprehensive Employment and Training Act. It traces the growth of the federal manpower system and the role played by the federal, state and local levels of government and private groups in shaping and implementing the system. After reviewing the manpower planning mechanism that developed during that decade, the several models which attempted to deliver comprehensive or consolidated manpower services are examined. Finally, the authors speculate about the future of manpower programs under the new CETA system.

129. Levy, Frank and Michael Wiseman. An Expanded Public Service Employment Program: Some Supply and Demand Considerations. Berkeley, California: Institute of Industrial Relations, 1971.

This study considers the capability of local government to expand employment of low-skilled workers through public service employment programs where such programs are defined as any policy designed to combat urban poverty through use of federal subsidies to increase employment of disadvantaged workers. The authors present a profile of workers in large U.S. metropolitan areas who earned less than $4,600 in 1966 and describe jobs provided by city government in Oakland and San Francisco, California, which could be held by such individuals. They address the problem of defining and estimating feasible expansions of "useful" city employment and conclude that such employment could be expanded 10-15% in low-skilled categories without severe disruption, costly additional inputs, and obvious makework.

130. Link, Charles R. Economic Impacts of a Particular Public Service Employment Program. Newark, Delaware: Delaware University Press, 1976. NTIS PB-257071/15T

The goal of this report is to shed light on the economic effects of a proposed Public Service Employment Program involving Unemployment Insurance (UI) exhaustees. The program is described and an empirical study determines the reservation wage of UI exhaustees by sex, race, education and age. The results suggest that the primary willing participants in a work relief program are low-educated black and white women with dependents. It is concluded that a Public Service Employment Program with a low wage rate would gain little support from exhaustees, regardless of race, education or number of dependents. Fragmentary evidence is presented which suggests the availability of a substantial number of jobs in the private sector that pay comparable wages. (NTIS)

131. Lipsman, Claire K. The Comprehensive Employment and Training Act: Abstracts of Selected Studies. Washington, D.C.: National Academy of Sciences, 1976.

This work encompasses a collection of abstracts of thirty-seven selected reports and papers related to CETA which includes most of the major policy, research and evaluation studies of CETA identified as of summer 1976. The abstracts which cover books, monographs, articles and papers are divided into three sections. The first includes all materials with a general or national frame of reference (10 abstracts). The second section includes studies concerned principally with specific geographic areas (10 abstracts). The last section consists of studies dealing primarily with a single topic related to CETA, for example, public employment, target groups or vocational education (17 abstracts).

132. McClure-Lundberg Associates. Business Involvement in CETA-The STIP Experience. Washington, D.C.: Employment and Training Administration, 1978. L37.2:B96

This booklet describes the Skill Training Improvement Program (STIP) which is a new approach to federally supported skill training founded on the close cooperation of the business and industrial community and the federal government. STIP is funded under Title III of CETA to provide advanced skill for unemployed and underemployed persons. Reports from five STIP programs are included to illustrate the range of program possibilities under STIP.

133. MacRae, C. Duncan, R. W. Crandall, and Ralph E. Smith. Wage Subsidy Research: Existing Models and Programs. Washington, D.C.: U.S. Department of Labor, 1972. NTIS PB253179/AS

This study examines the effects of the Work Incentive (WIN) Program tax credit on the market for WIN participants and on the markets for other labor. Existing economic theory is used for a comparative analysis of wage, training, and income subsidies. Additionally, the simulation models of a universal wage-rate subsidy and an employment training tax credit are examined, and the experience of existing wage-related subsidy programs, Job Opportunities in the Business Sector (JOBS), and the experimental Training Incentives Payments Program (TIPP) reviewed.

Finally, the effect of the WIN tax credit is inferred from an econometric model of the demand for low-skill labor. The analysis reveals that the administrator of the WIN tax credit program, in general, faces the dilemma of increasing employment of subsidized WIN workers while displacing unsubsidized low-skill workers or increasing the earnings of those WIN participants who would have been employed without the tax credit by raising job standards. Other inferences are limited by the static nature of the models available. (ASPER)

134. Mangum, Garth L. Employability, Employment and Income. Salt Lake City, Utah: Olympus Press, 1976.

This book attempts to reassess U.S. manpower policies of the past fifteen years. It seeks to define manpower policy in the context of what lies ahead in the last quarter of the twentieth century, and by isolating the social and economic factors which affected

manpower policies in the 1950's and 1960's. The author establishes
some basic premises of labor market operation, identifies forces of
change (economic, demographic and social) which will require U.S.
manpower policies to change accordingly, and indicates the labor
market malfunctions toward which future manpower policies should be
directed.

This analysis serves as a base from which various policy alternatives are developed and is used to gauge the potential of the
various alternatives. The conclusion of the work includes the
author's recommendation of the policy changes which correspond most
promisingly with the aforementioned labor market malfunctions.

135. Mangum, Garth L., David Snedeker and Bonnie Snedeker. Self-Evalua-
tion of CETA Manpower Programs: A Guide for Prime Sponsors. Washington,
D. C.: Employment and Training Administration, 1976. L37.8/2:SP6

This guide was prepared to aid prime sponsor staffs, directors, and
advisory council members in understanding the role and process of
program evaluation. The work is based on a review of evaluation
activities conducted by selected prime sponsors, a review of
evaluation literature and consultation with prime sponsor staffs
involved in local evaluations. The study emphasizes that, at a
time when most prime sponsors have limited experience in managing
programs, the first concern should be operational control and
monitoring. Then, as sound reporting and monitoring systems are
developed, effectiveness evaluation becomes the next priority. The
report concludes with a review of the methodologies, complexities
and limitations of various evaluation efforts which prime sponsors
should consider in their program evaluation efforts.

136. Mangum, Garth L. and John Walsh. A Decade of Manpower Development
and Training. Salt Lake City, Utah, Olympus Press, 1973.

Mangum and Walsh evaluate the ten-year experience of the Manpower
Development and Training Act (MDTA), less from attack or defense of
a particular program than as an assessment of the economic and
social role of an adult remedial skills training activity. The
authors review the conditions and premises from which it emerged
and note the major policy changes which affected both its nature
and its objective. In the final chapter, conclusions and recommendations are given based on the evaluation.

137. Manpower Development Corporation, Inc. How to Get Started on
Evaluation: A Field Report and Guide for CETA Prime Sponsors. Washington, D.C.: Employment and Training Administration, 1977. L37.8:Evl

Based on work done by MDC, Inc., this report provides a working
guide to local evaluation of employment and training programs as a
means of improving programs and as a planning tool. It is designed
for CETA prime sponsors and program operators who have little experience in evaluation or sufficient staff for extensive evaluations. Two techniques, one which attempts to determine what is
happening in an employment and training program and the second
which attempts to determine to the extent feasible why that is hap-

pening, are outlined. A case study of Escambia County, Florida completes the report.

138. Manpower Development Corporation, Inc. The Planning and Implementation of CETA Title VI: PSE Expansion Projects Under the Economic Stimulus Act of 1977, Vol. II: Detailed Findings. Chapel Hill, North Carolina: Manpower Development Corporation, 1978.

See abstract under Autry, George (#9).

139. Martin, Philip L. "Public Service Employment and Rural America," American Journal of Agricultural Economics, 59, May, 1977, pp. 278-282.

Public Service Employment (PSE) programs are manpower instruments that provide income and transitional employment in times of high unemployment. Despite annual fund expenditures of nearly $1 billion since 1971, little attention has been directed toward the rural-urban distribution of Public Employment funds. After establishing alternative allocation formulae, actual allocations are compared with hypothetical allocations for public employment programs since 1971. The results indicate that rural areas did not obtain Public Employment funds in proportion to their shares of total unemployment. Reasons for the observed pattern of allocations are explored, and alternative allocating criteria to increase funds available to rural areas are discussed. (ERIC)

140. Masters, Stanley. "The Effects of Supported Work on the Earnings and Transfer Payments of its AFDC Target Group," Journal of Human Resources, 16, Fall, 1981, pp. 600-636.

The effects of supported work on a sample of 1,620 long-term AFDC recipients are analyzed in this paper. The author finds positive, statistically significant effects on the postprogram earnings of experimentals. Although the experimental effect declines sharply over time at one of seven sites, at the others the effect increases somewhat faster than the rate of inflation. The postprogram effects are concentrated disproportionately in public-sector employment but not in CETA/WIN positions. The increased earnings of experimentals leads to significant payment reductions in welfare. In the long run, the author estimates that the experimental effect on earnings will be $53 per month for earnings and $22 per month for disposable income. (JHR)

141. Mathematica Policy Research, Inc. Evaluation of the Economic Impact of the Job Corps Program. Washington, D. C.: Mathematica Policy Research, 1978.

This report presents the first post-program findings of a study designed to provide a comprehensive evaluation of the short-term impacts of the Job Corps program. It is based on detailed interviews with program participants and a comparison group conducted in 1977 and reinterviews nine months later with participants who had been out of the program for over five months and all comparison group members. The study found that Job Corps participants had greater earnings gains than nonparticipants with those who completed the program experiencing the greatest gains. Program

participants, particularly completers, also did better than the
nonparticipants in other areas such as employment, further education, mobility, health, welfare participation, arrests, and drug
and alcohol abuse. Seven months after leaving the program, most
participants expressed overall satisfaction with their experience
although most were critical of job placement assistance. The
study's cost-benefit analysis of the Job Corps indicates that
benefits do exceed program costs.

142. Mathematica Policy Research, Inc. Targeting CETA and Single Heads
of Families. Washington, D.C.: Mathematica Policy Research, 1979.

The 1978 reauthorization of CETA called for an examination of the
impacts of CETA eligibility regulations on single heads of house-
holds. This study examines the impacts of the new CETA regulations
in terms of the degree to which CETA services address the income
and labor market needs of single heads of families, the targeting
of CETA eligibility on single family heads, the impacts of targeted
eligibility on the pattern of participation rates and the degree to
which CETA services solve the income maintenance and labor market
needs of single heads of families. It finds that problems exist
for single family heads relative to nonsingle family heads when
official measures of economic disadvantage are used, particularly
for displaced homemakers. The problems include restricted eligibility and only a modest targeting of special interest groups such
as welfare recipients, older Americans, women and heads of low-
income families. The report concludes with suggestions for change.

143. Mattson, Robert E. An Evaluation of Individual and Pool Slot
Development for Public Service Employment: The Vermont Experience.
Montpelier, Vermont: Vermont State Employment Service, 1973. NTIS
PB231850/9

Public Service Employment slots can be developed in three ways:
(1) by establishing a pool of jobs into which trainees can be
placed; (2) by developing individualized slots for each trainee;
(3) by combining the pool and individualized approaches. In terms
of administrative and cost efficiency there is little difference
between the pool and the individualized approach. The pool
approach has several drawbacks from the employer's standpoint: (1)
some slots may be unfilled for long periods of time; (2) some slots
may be negotiated with the business manager, leaving the supervisor
somewhat in the dark until the trainees are on the job and ready
for his supervision. In terms of client outcomes, those in individualized slots are more likely to complete training, but there is
no significant difference between the two groups in the rate of
permanent placement. The best method of slot development is
probably "individualized placement" within a pool of slots. (ERIC)

144. Mattson, Robert E. and Joseph A. Rution. Considerations in the
Selections of Public Service Employers: The Vermont Experience.
Montpelier, Vermont: Vermont State Employment Service, 1973. NTIS
PB-231854/1

In a Public Service Employment Program of subsidized work training,
nonprofit employers in the areas of health, education, social

services and government can be evaluated in terms of the client's employability growth, wages, supervision, retention, transferability, and client satisfaction. Client employability is observed to increase in all four areas of employment, though slowly for classroom and day care aides. Wage levels are in the $2.00 to $2.40 range--highest for municipal employees, lowest for paraprofessional aides, with clericals in the middle. Clients seemed generally satisfied with their jobs and with the supervision in all four areas. Retention is especially high in health, higher education, and government, owing to large payroll, high turnover, wide job variety, reliable budgeting, and favorable employer attitude toward the program. Retention seems to be low for classroom and day care aides because there are few openings, little turnover, and a tight job market restricts transferability. (ERIC)

145. Maxfield, Max, Jr., David Edson, Fredric Raines and Barbara Delaney. Open Ended Public Service Employment Programs: The JOBS Microsimulation Model. Washington, D.C.: U.S. Department of Labor, 1979. NTIS PB293205/AS

This final report, consisting of several documents by different authors, constructs a model of welfare programs which produces estimates of the budgetary costs and caseloads of alternative hypothesized programs. The first paper, by Myles Maxfield, presents an overview of the project, including the main policy issues addressed and the principal features and results of the Job Opportunities in the Business Sector (JOBS) model. A microsimulation model of employment-related welfare reform programs is constructed. It focuses on the decision of eligible persons to apply for public service employment. Their decision is based on an explicit treatment of employment and income expectations and of the monetary value of nonmarket time. Estimates of the caseload of the Program for Better Jobs and Income (PBJI) are produced. The second paper, by David Edson, discusses a specific application of the JOBS model to the administration's PBJI. The author computes transfer payments, predicts participation behavior of individuals and families, and aggregates program caseload by summing over the sample of microdata. The report estimates that PBJI increases costs by 75-percent relative to current AFDC, SSI, and Food Stamp programs. This estimate includes cash assistance for 15 million families and a public service employment program providing a full year equivalent of 1.7 million jobs. The paper by Fredric Raines hypothesizes a model in which reservation wages are determined by the demand for leisure, the duration of employment, and home productivity. The author also uses a model estimated with regression analysis using the self-reported reservation wages from the National Longitudinal Surveys. Results confirm the hypothesis. The predicted values are used in the microsimulation model.

Barbara Delaney uses the model to examine the determinants of the time allocated for men. Based on data from the Panel Survey of Income Dynamics, the empirical analysis suggests that the market labor supply of men is very insensitive to nonmarket characteristics.

This study was a basic resource in formulating the Administration's 1978 proposal for a "Program for Better Jobs and Income." (ASPER)

146. Meigs, Jo. Federal Manpower Programs: The Need for Experimental Design. Washington, D.C.: U.S. Department of Labor, 1975. NTIS PB266047/AS

This paper sets forth the principles of experimental research design to evaluate the effectiveness of manpower programs designed to increase the participants' earnings, wage rates, and job security. Several less effective approaches are presented for comparison, to illustrate their inadequacies.

Programs should be initially designed as experiments (or have experimental components) to facilitate evaluation. An intentionally experimental approach would afford the opportunity to learn faster by trying alternative concepts simultaneously and would increase the likelihood that one could determine not only that a particular concept failed, but also why it failed. Unless studies are conducted systematically, the conditions under which a particular method is most useful will not be learned. Much improvement is still needed before policymakers will allow this research to be a crucial part of the decision-making process. (ASPER)

147. Mirengoff, William and Lester Rindler. CETA: Manpower Programs Under Local Control. Washington D. C.: National Academy of Sciences, 1978.

This work represents the final report of a study conducted by the Committee on Evaluation and Training Programs, seeking to assess the impact of CETA on manpower programs. The report examines the differences between CETA Title I programs and their predecessors and compares legislative goals with results. It also examines the impact of Public Service Employment programs on the structurally oriented programs of Title I and the degree to which the primary objective of Title V (creation of new jobs) is achieved. The first of the report's ten chapters provides an overview of CETA history, a summary of CETA objectives, and a summary of the evaluation committee's conclusions in relation to accomplishments, problems, recommendations, and policy issues. Chapters two to nine discuss the major findings under the following categories: Resources and Allocations, Manpower Planning, Administration, Program Choices, the Delivery of Title I Services, Public Service Employment, Clientele, and Program Effectiveness. The last chapter summarizes the major findings and recommendations under the following topics: Allocation of Resources, Substantive Aspects of CETA Programs, Administrative Processes, and Institutional Relationships. Included in the appendixes are: a glossary of Manpower acronyms, the calculation formula for the job creation ratio, recommendations made by the National Commission for Manpower Policy, and statistical tables. (NTIS)

148. Mirengoff, William, Lester Rindler, Harry Greenspan and Scott Seablom. CETA: Assessment of Public Service Employment Programs. Washington, D.C.: National Academy of Sciences, 1979.

This study is part of a CETA evaluation series undertaken by the Committee on Evaluation of Employment and Training Programs established by the National Research Council in 1974 to assess the social, economic and political effects of CETA legislation. It analyzes the extent to which targeting objectives of the Emergency Jobs Program Extension Act (EJPEA) of 1976 have been achieved and the effectiveness of limited duration projects in providing useful public services. The study deals with the administration and program delivery of EJPEA and with the consequences of doubling the size of public service employment programs in a very short period. It examines whether jobs created are positions that would not otherwise exist, but does not assess the extent of substitution. As in the earlier studies, the major source of data was a survey conducted through a network of field research associates in 28 areas.

149. Mirengoff, William, Lester Rindler, Harry Greenspan, Scott Seablom and Lois Black. The New CETA: Effect on Public Service Employment Programs. Washington D. C.: National Academy of Sciences, 1980.

The 1978 reauthorization amendments were intended to rectify CETA's shortcomings and hence established "The New CETA". This study provides a preliminary assessment of the effects of such legislative amendments on the PSE programs in terms of eligibility and wage provisions, planning and management systems, administrative processes and institutional relationships. Targeting and wage restrictions seem to be relatively successful whereas the CETA administration appears to have become more difficult and burdensome. The authors conclude that is too soon to assess transition outcomes, however they do present some issues for further investigation, including the relationship between CETA and the welfare system.

150. Mirengoff, William, et al. Expanding Public Service Employment Under CETA: Preliminary Assessment. Washington, D.C.: National Research Council, 1978.

This report provides an early assessment of the 1977 implementation of the revised and expanded public service employment (PSE) program of the Comprehensive Employment and Training Act (CETA). It focuses on actions taken by local and state governments (prime sponsors) to meet the pressure for a large increase in PSE as part of the 1977 countercyclical employment expansion policy. It finds that the goal of employing over 400,000 additional unemployed workers in PSE jobs was accomplished in the scheduled nine months, but that the emphasis and speed was at the expense of some design elements. It discusses in some detail the changing characteristics of participants, the nature of work performed, and the response of the CETA system to the demand for rapid implementation of a large new program. (NTIS)

151. Moayed-Dadkhah, Kamran. Cost Analysis of OEO-ORI Longitudinal Study of Four Manpower Programs. Washington, D.C.: U.S. Department of Labor, 1975. NTIS PB267769/AS

The purpose of this study was to analyze the costs of four employment and training programs examined in the four manpower programs
evaluation study (see contract J-9-M-6-0095): (1) Neighborhood
Youth Corps/ Out of School Component (NYC/OS), (2) Job Corps, (3)
Job Opportunities in the Business Sector (JOBS), and (4) Manpower
Development and Training Act-Institutional Program (MDTA). Within
a conventional economic cost framework, data were collected and
analyzed using regression analysis. Each of the four programs was
examined separately and tests were made to see if variants within
each program had different cost functions.

The most important finding was that data for three of the four
programs displayed sufficient regularity to make the existence of a
cost function plausible. But the JOBS program exhibited no dis-
cernible relationship between output and costs, making both understanding and oversight of the program difficult. The other three
programs all had well-defined cost functions, although of quite
different shape. For NYC/OS as a whole, marginal cost increased
slowly throughout the whole range of output levels. For the Job
Corps and MDTA, marginal cost was found to be constant. None of
the within-program tests on program variations revealed any significant differences. Although economics suggests there should be a
point at which average cost is a minimum, this point could not be
found for any of the programs. This may reflect insufficient
variation within the programs to allow estimation of the rather
complicated functions necessary to find such minimum cost points.
(ASPER)

152. Moayed-Dadkhah, Kamran and Ernst W. Stromsdorfer. Cost Analysis of
Manpower Programs: An Analysis of the State of the Art. Washington,
D.C.: U.S. Department of Labor, 1973. NTIS PB256337/AS

This survey of the literature of cost analysis employed in evaluation studies of employment and training programs reveals that the
four issues that analysts found most difficult were: (1) the
distinction between capital and variable costs; (2) the conversion
of financial data into economic costs; (3) the estimation of cost
functions; and (4) the estimation of foregone earnings of trainees.
Considerable confusion also existed over the nature and treatment
of transfer payments.

It was found that the proper treatment of transfer payments, income
and social security taxes, trainee allowances, foregone earnings,
or post-training earnings depends on the locus of optimization one
is concerned with, but is critical on both efficiency and equity
grounds.

The poor quality of some of the earlier studies demonstrates the
evolution of cost analysis methodology, the lack of convertibility
of Federal accounting data, and the failure of economists to use
appropriate methodology and to conceptualize the problem of cost
measurement as one wherein costs are related to outputs via a
production function.

After exploring the problems encountered in measuring the costs of
employment and training programs caused by the nature of the data

reporting process itself--problems related to definitions, the administrative process, procedural anomalies, different program institutional contexts, and errors in the data and deviations from reporting procedures--the researchers conclude that some relatively minor standardization of cost and output measures, with considerable disaggregation in reporting, could turn the government's data set into an evaluative component of considerable value. (ASPER)

153. Morlock, Mark J. Public Service Employment: The Impact on Washington State's Nonmetropolitan Labor Markets. Washington, D.C.: GPO, 1980. A1.36:1619

A Public Service Employment (PSE) program that provided work for the unemployed was found to have improved the status of workers in the Washington State job market during fiscal year 1976. Nonmetropolitan county unemployment rates dropped an average 0.5 percent; post-program wages increased 82 cents per hour for women and 99 cents for men in unsubsidized employment; and job skills improved, usually in proportion with years of education. PSE may serve as a valuable manpower development tool in nonmetropolitan areas, though some drawbacks include underutilization of skills, overconcentrations of participants with higher levels of education, and weak training for the disadvantaged worker. (ERIC)

154. Nadworny, M. J., R. B. Lawson and R. E. Musty. Financial Disincentives for Welfare Clients to Enter Public Service Employment: The Vermont Experience. Montpelier, Vermont: Vermont Department of Employment Security, 1973. NTIS PB-231899/6GI

From a comparative economic viewpoint--does regular employment secured through temporary subsidized special work training, afford the publicly supported individual any marginal advantage over his welfare status? A study of 279 ANFC recipients was conducted to address this question. The median annual dollar value of tax-free welfare payments in Vermont was $4,075. When combined with Medicaid and Food Stamp bonuses, this was equivalent to a $4,465 taxable income for the family unit. Given the median $2.26 hourly rate wage realized by program enrollees, male ANFC clients experienced an economic disincentive to work. Females improved their welfare status modestly when allowed certain income exemptions. Real income rose sharply for the study group only during special work training. When a graduated welfare support schedule was combined with a subsidized wage program, per capita income rose to $6,793. Otherwise, there was no real financial incentive to leave welfare status. (NTIS)

155. Nathan, Richard P. Monitoring the Public Service Employment Program: The Second Round. Washington, D.C.: Brookings Institution, 1979.

This study, undertaken for the National Commission for Employment Policy, is based on two rounds of field observations by a network of twenty-six social science researchers who studied a stratified sample of forty-one governmental jurisdictions representing thirty-one CETA prime sponsors. The report presents data and findings for the second round of field research. It is a continuation of the

project entitled "Job Creation Through Public Service Employment"
sponsored by the National Commission for Manpower Policy. Third
round results are expected in late 1981.

156. Nathan, Richard P., Robert F. Cook, V. Lane Rawlings and Associates. Public Service Employment: A Field Evaluation. Washington,
D.C.: Brookings Institution, 1981.

This book presents an overview of the methodology and a discussion
of the results from the first two rounds of the Brookings monitoring study of CETA-PSE programs. It is based on the detailed
project description and results contained in Nathan, Job Creation
through Public Service Employment and Nathan, Monitoring the Public
Service Employment Program: Second Round, both of which are included in this bibliography. In addition to the discussion of
results from the Brookings Study of PSE programs, this volume also
contains a chapter "Subsidizing Employment in the Nonprofit Sector"
by Janet Galchick and Michael Wiseman. This section concerns the
use of nonprofit agencies in the PSE program. For details see the
abstract under Galchick in this bibliography.

157. Nathan, Richard P., et al. Job Creation Through Public Service
Employment. Washington, D.C.: National Commission for Manpower Policy,
1978. Y3.N31: 1/6/V1-3

Abstract: See National Commission for Manpower Policy (#164).

158. National Academy of Sciences. CETA: Assessment and Recommendations. Washington, D.C.: National Academy of Sciences, 1978.

This is one of a series of studies of CETA by the Committee on
Evaluation of Employment and Training Programs (CEETP). The
monograph begins with a brief history of CETA and its objectives.
It follows with the results of a study of 28 prime sponsors that
lists the issues, findings, and recommendations of the CEETP in the
areas of allocation of resources, substantive aspects of CETA
programs (who should be served, program mix, program results and
other), administrative processes and institutional relationships.
Included in the work is an appendix with an index of manpower
acronyms.

159. National Academy of Sciences. Employment and Training Programs:
The Local View. Washington, D.C.: National Academy of Sciences, 1978.

This volume contains nine case studies describing the initial
two-year experiences of local governments implementing the Comprehensive Employment and Training Act of 1973. An earlier volume
published eight similar area studies on the transition from federally centralized to decentralized manpower programs. Written by
resident field researchers familiar with the local scene, these
reports span a range of experiences from well-run operations to one
on the verge of dissolution (because of interjurisdictional ten-
sions). The reports are approximately twenty pages in length and
summarize how local governments administer employability development and Public Service Employment programs. Specific topics
covered include: (1) pre-CETA services; (2) the clientele served;

(3) relationship with other state and local agencies; (4) assessment of program effectiveness; and (5) the planning and administration of Titles I, II, and VI. Problems such as piecemeal planning and difficulty in arranging on-the-job training are discussed. The overall tenor of the studies is positive, reflecting progress in coordinating local program operations. (ERIC)

160. National Academy of Sciences. Final Report of the Panel on Manpower Training Evaluation: The Use of Social Security Earnings Data for Assessing the Impact of Manpower Training Programs. Washington, D.C.: U.S. Department of Labor, 1974. NTIS PB254938/AS

To evaluate the educational or economic effects of government training programs inexpensively, reliably, and currently, this study proposes the use of Social Security Continuous Work History Sample (CWHS) data. It explains the current structure of Social Security data available for evaluation of training programs, compares CWHS data with alternative data sets and discusses the advantages and disadvantages of using the data.

CWHS data are judged to be inexpensive, reliable, and longitudinal; the sample is large; nonresponse is not a problem; and comparison groups are included. However, the study points out that the data show earnings rather than wage rates and hours of work, lack detailed information on labor force participation, do not report earnings for those earning above the maximum, vary in coverage as a function of age, have a time lag, cover a limited number of socio-demographic variables, and involve problems with maintaining confidentiality. Nevertheless, the report recommends that CWHS data be more widely used to evaluate manpower training programs, that strict controls be placed to maintain confidentiality of the data, that the Manpower Automated Reporting System (MARS) file be evaluated to determine and reduce nonreporting biases, and that a study be undertaken to determine the validity of Social Security data for manpower program evaluation. (ASPER)

161. National Commission for Manpower Policy. CETA: An Analysis of the Issues. Washington, D.C.: National Commission for Manpower Policy, 1978. Y3.M31: 9/23

This report presents an overview of CETA programs summarizing titles in terms of purpose, eligibility, funding, services, and delivery. In addition, the issues of targeting, program outcomes, funding and information systems are considered in detail.

162. National Commission for Manpower Policy. Community Based Organizations in Manpower Programs and Policy, Special Report No. 16. Washington, D.C.: National Commission for Manpower Policy, 1977. Y3.M31: 9/16

The role of Community Based Organizations (CBO's) in CETA is the focus of this report. A background paper entitled "The Role of Community Based Organizations in Manpower Policy and Programs" by Maurice A. Dawkins is included as well as a summary of the conference discussions. The major areas of concern to emerge from the conference include the ambiguity of officials to CBO's, the political issues involved in funding which bypassed local elected officials and funneled directly to CBO's, and the seeming unrealistic criteria with which CBO's have to contend.

163. National Commission for Manpower Policy. Current Issues in the Relationship Between Manpower Research and Policy, Special Report No. 7. Washington, D.C.: National Commission for Manpower Policy, 1976. Y3.M31: 9/7

A summary of a conference held to consider current issues in the role research, evaluation and experimentation have played in manpower policy. The conference report includes a background paper by Herbert S. Parnes entitled "The National Longitudinal Survey: Lessons for Human Resources Policy." In this paper, the author reviews the National Longitudinal Study begun in 1966, including the findings and paper resulting from the study. He concludes that human resource policy in the U.S. has suffered from inadequate attention to the demand side, inadequate emphasis to long-run compared to short-run programs on the supply side, and an inadequate integration of human resources policy. In addition to this background paper, the report provides a summary of the conference discussion and selected comments on the paper and the conference.

164. National Commission for Manpower Policy. Job Creation Through Public Service Employment; Volume 1, Summary of Findings and Recommendations; Volume 2, Monitoring the Public Service Employment Program; Volume 3, Commissioned Papers. Washington, D.C.: National Commission for Manpower Policy, 1978. Y3.M31: 1/6/V.1-3

The first volume contains the findings and recommendations of the National Commission for Manpower Policy on the net effects of Public Service Employment (PSE). This document is divided into four sections. Section 1 includes the letter of transmittal sent to Congress and a summary of the findings. Section 2 contains a full report of the Commission's findings and recommendations with respect to the role of PSE in national manpower policy and programming, the net employment effects of PSE, and the future of PSE. Section 3 provides an overview of the issues and evidence of PSE. This section contains a brief description of the historical antecedents, identifies the various objectives which PSE has been intended to serve and evaluates the success of the program in achieving each of these objectives, identifies the problems involved in implementing the program through a decentralized delivery system, and summarizes the issues considered by the Commission. The fourth section contains the Commission's field reviews of PSE. It summarizes the four reviews under the following general headings: The Net Employment Effects of PSE; Targeting, Training, and Transition; Wages and Output; Program Administration; Community Organizations; and Future Directions for PSE.

The second volume contains the interim report of the Brookings Institution to the Commission based on their on-site monitoring of the program. The report is divided into seven chapters. Chapter 1 provides an overview of the report, and Chapter 2 presents a brief history of the PSE programs. Chapter 3 discusses employment effects. (An understanding of the definitions of job creation and displacement used in this chapter is crucial to the interpretation of the extent of displacement found in this study.) Chapter 4 examines the fiscal consequences of the PSE program for governmental jurisdictions participating in it. Chapter 5 addresses the programmatic and social effects of the program and includes an analysis of the functional areas in which PSE participants are employed, their occupations, social characteristics, and wages. The political effects of PSE are examined in Chapter 6 which describes the organization and administration of the program at the local level. Finally, Chapter 7 discusses the policy implications of the current findings.

The third volume contains papers prepared for the commission's use by various scholars in the field. The four papers in this volume are: John Palmer, "Evaluating the Economic Stimulus Package from an Employment and Training Perspective;" Martin Neil Baily and Robert M. Solow, "Public Service Employment as Macroeconomic Policy;" Michael Borus and Daniel Hamermesh, "Study of the Net Employment Effects of Public Service Employment--Econometric Analyses;" Harry Katz and Michael Wiseman, "An Essay on Subsidized Employment in the Public Sector." Each of these papers is abstracted separately in this bibliography by the author. (ERIC)

165. National Commission for Manpower Policy. Manpower Program Coordination, Special Report No. 2. Washington, D.C.: National Commission for Manpower Policy, 1975. Y3M31: 9/2

This report is based on initial studies of manpower program coordination conducted by the National Commission for Manpower Policy as created under CETA Title V. Manpower coordination has four facets to it, namely: policy, planning, administration and program. This study analyzes planning, information exchange and technical assistance needs at the local, state and federal levels. A number of recommendations are developed that can lead to improved conditions. In particular, it is concluded that coordination should evolve as a continuing activity to support the development of a national manpower policy, and that policy coordination will be the focus of the future.

166. National Commission for Manpower Policy. Proceedings of a Conference on Public Service Employment, Special Report No. 1. Washington, D.C.: National Commission for Manpower Policy, 1975. Y3.M31: 9/1

This report summarizes a conference on Public Service Employment. Included are background papers prepared for the conference by Robert E. Hall, "The Role of Public Service Employment in Federal Unemployment Policy"; Richard P. Nathan, "Public Service Employment--'Compared to What'"; Alan E. Fechter, "Public Service Employment: Boon or Boondoggle?"; and Sar A. Levitan, "Creation of Jobs for the Unemployed". In addition to these four background papers, written comments and the views of invited interest groups are included. These all serve as the basis for an "Issue Paper on Public Service Employment and Job Creation" prepared by the commission's staff.

167. National Commission for Manpower Policy. Public Service Employment and Other Responses to Continued Unemployment. Washington, D.C.: National Commission for Manpower Policy, 1975. Y3M31: 1/2

> This report summarizes the findings and recommendations on PSE along with considering other responses to continuing unemployment. This booklet's content is presented in two sections. Section 1 summarizes the findings and makes twenty-one recommendations pertaining to PSE, summer jobs for youth, the unemployment insurance system, special assistance to the unemployed (mortgage payments and health insurance), energy and its manpower implications, and coordination of manpower and related programs. The second section discusses the assumptions, expectations and concerns which led to the recommendations presented in section 1. (ERIC)

168. National League of Cities. Youth Knowledge Development Report: CETA Youth Programs in Small Cities. Washington, D.C.: GPO, 1980. L37.19/2:3.18

> Although two-fifths of the poor live outside metropolitan areas and three-fifths outside central cities of 50,000 or more, CETA legislation makes certain implicit assumptions which orients the program toward larger metropolitan areas. In addition, to be eligible for direct funding, a prime sponsor must represent an area with a population of at least 100,000.

> Because of this situation, a study was undertaken by the National League of Cities to review the youth program experience in small cities. The review suggests that in these areas there is inadequate involvement of local decision-makers and that complex administrative procedures often stand in the way of mounting effective programs. In addition, constraints on activities such as inadequate transportation, limitations in the diversity of potential work and training sites, categorization of programs, unrealistic wage standards and inadequate information from the Department of Labor present significant problems. This report suggests ways of addressing these problems.

169. The National Manpower Policy Task Force, The Best Way to Reduce Unemployment is to Create More Jobs. Washington, D. C.: GPO, 1975.

> This policy statement expresses the need for the federal government to reduce unemployment through direct and indirect job creation. The authors recommend various job creation strategies and evaluate each separately. Although no single approach can offer a panacea, the benefits derived from federal government job creation are deemed to far outweigh the costs.

170. National Planning Association. An Evaluation of the Economic Impact Project of the Public Employment Program, Volume I. Washington, D.C.: National Planning Association, 1974. PB-236 892/6GI

> Two sets of demonstration projects were established. The first, the Welfare Demonstration Projects, was designed to test the effectiveness of a public employment program carried out at a fairly large scale with special emphasis on employable AFDC welfare

recipients. The second set of demonstrations--referred to as the High Impact Demonstrations was designed to test the consequences of a large-scale public employment program carried out under the same general regulations and guidelines as the regular program. Both sets of demonstrations were implemented in the same five states-- California, Illinois, New Jersey, New York, and South Carolina--but in different cities and counties. (NTIS)

171. National Planning Association. An Evaluation of the Economic Impact Project of the Public Employment Program, Volume II. Washington, D.C.: National Planning Association, 1974. PB-236 893/4GI

The report is volume two, of a four volume evaluation study, which is an appendix to volume one of the study and provides supplemental detail on the following subjects: background and guidelines of the Emergency Employment Act of 1971; Administrative structure of the high impact demonstration projects; hiring procedures in the demon- stration sites; training provided to PEP participants; community response to PEP; PEP as transitional employment. (NTIS)

172. National Planning Association. An Evaluation of the Economic Impact Project of the Public Employment Program, Volume III. Washing- ton, D.C.: National Planning Association, 1974. PB-236 894/2GI

The report is volume three, of a four volume evaluation study, which is an appendix to volume one of the study and provides sup- plemental data on the following subject: factors associates with participants pre and post program income and labor market status; a labor flow model based on PEP; the net government job creation effect; case studies of the sites involved. (NTIS)

173. National Planning Association. An Evaluation of the Economic Impact Project of the Public Employment Program, Volume IV. Washington, D.C.: National Planning Association, 1974. PB-236 895/9GI

The report is volume four, of a four volume evaluation study, which is an appendix to volume one of the study and provides supplemental data on the following subjects: local economic changes and the high impact; data sources and reliability; survey instruments. (NTIS)

174. Northrup, Herbert R., Richard C. Rowan, Bernard E. Anderson and John E. Welsh. Feasibility Study to Develop a Model for Furthering the Involvement of Private Indus try with CETA Sponsors Especially in Train- ing and Placement. Philadelphia, Pennsylvania: Industrial Research Unit, The Wharton School, University of Pennsylvania, 1977.

This study finds little systematic relationship between the nature and extent of business participation on CETA advisory councils and the cooperation of the private sector with CETA prime sponsors in job placement and skills training. Neither increased representa- tion on the council nor more active participation by business representatives seems to influence significantly the rate of private industry placement of CETA trainees. One of the major factors influencing the relationship between prime sponsors and the business community is the prevailing political climate.

In addition, the study shows the critical role of CETA planning staffs in forging a link between prime sponsors and the private sector; however, the communication between CETA planners and business representatives is generally less than adequate.

An assessment of the occupational skills training received under the various CETA programs indicates that the relative quality of training improves as the direct involvement of private employers in providing the training is increased. The privately operated and CETA funded institutional training programs seem to be the most successful occupational training programs analyzed during this study. The model set forth is based upon these findings.

175. Pacific Consultants, Camil Associates and Ketron. The Impact of WIN II. Washington, D.C.: Employment and Training Administration, 1976. NTIS PB-261 277/8GA

An evaluation of WIN II is undertaken, based on the success of the individual participants in the program in terms of placement and welfare reduction. The impact evaluation stresses the differences in job search duration and earnings between (a) what participants actually experienced and (b) what they would have experienced in the absence of WIN. For that purpose a control group of applicants/ nonparticipants was used. Both groups were interviewed three times, thus the assessment effort was undertaken longitudinally where changes in participants' status can be noted. Moreover, the issue of "benefit decay" is analyzed. Finally, the labor market conditions of the period under consideration are thoroughly analyzed in order to control outside influences and isolate the pure WIN benefits.

176. Palmer, John L., (editor). Creating Jobs: Public Employment Programs and Wage Subsidies. Washington, D.C.: Brookings Institution, 1978.

This volume presents the results of a Brookings conference convened to assess the effects of proposals which involve direct intervention of the federal government in the job market. A summary of the principal findings is followed by seven papers with commentaries. These papers suggest a variety of ways for estimating how public-employment and wage subsidy schemes would affect unemployment and the economy. Three of the papers estimate the impact of job creating action, three deal with the application of policy in different times and places, and one simulates a guaranteed employment program.

177. Parnes, Herbert S. "The National Longitudinal Survey: Lessons for Human Resources Policy," in National Commission for Manpower Policy. Current Issues in the Relationship Between Manpower Research and Policy, Special Report No. 7. Washington, D.C.: National Commission for Manpower Policy, 1976. Y3.M31: 9/7

See abstract under National Commission for Manpower Policy (#163).

178. Perry, Charles, et. al. The Impact of Government Manpower Programs. Philadelphia: The Industrial Relations Unit, The Wharton
School, The University of Pennsylvania, 1975.

The identification and documentation of the impact of employment
and training programs on participants with particular attention to
minorities and women is undertaken in this volume. A review of 252
previous studies combined with an analysis of program operating
statistics including enrollee data and completion status form the
basis of this analysis.

The work is divided into two parts. Part one compares eleven
employment and training programs. Because these programs present a
mosaic of goals, organizational structure and participant characteristics, they are classifed in four categories based on their
service mix and short-term economic impact. The four categories
are: (1) skill training, (2) job development, (3) employability
development, and (4) work experience. Based on this classification
the conceptual and methodological issues associated with evaluation
of the impacts of employment and training programs are discussed
and both economic effects (earnings, wage rates, employment
stability) and non-economic effects (attitude, job satisfaction)
outlined.

Part two analyzes each employment and training program separately
in terms of program history, scope, objectives and impact. The
findings reveal that skill training had greater economic impact
than the other categories of programs, participation by minorities
and women was significant and non-economic benefits represent
important impacts of employment and training programs but data on
such impacts are limited. Finally, suggestions for future research
are made with particular attention to the data base required for
such research.

179. Pierson, Frank C. The Minimum Level of Unemployment and Public
Policy. Kalamazoo, Michigan: W. E. Upjohn Institute for Employment
Research, 1980.

Persistent high levels of structural unemployment in periods of
relatively high employment are attributable to structural imbal-
ances in the economy. This structural unemployment is confined to
certain groups, including those with low incomes, few skills and
little education. In addition, it has a distinct geographical
bias. In the face of these factors, this study focuses on the role
of public policy in reducing the unemployment rate during periods
of relatively high employment. The traditional reliance on aggregate demand policies--monetary and fiscal policies--to solve
problems of unemployment tends to be inflationary and have limited
impact in the economically disadvantaged. Yet those traditional
policies are required for short-run stabilization purposes. Thus,
the critical issue is to balance the short-run needs with the
long-run goals of the economy when selecting public policy alternatives.

For the problem of structural unemployment, policies must consider
the particular needs of each subgroup and provide linkages between

education, training and employers. To do this, the serious barriers faced by the structurally unemployed including disincentives to work associated with nonwork sources of income, discrimination in hiring and promoting deficiencies in general education and training, and the lack of work experience must be considered. If the structurally unemployed are to achieve job-readiness status, major changes in the nation's public school system are required as are improvements in the levels of training available. In addition, long-term efforts to attack other barriers are desirable if the unemployment rate is to be permanently reduced.

180. Pines, Marion W. and James H. Morlock. <u>Work Experience Perspectives: CETA Program Models</u>. Washington, D.C.: Employment and Training Administration, 1979. L37.8/6: W89/979

Understanding the potential of work experience activity as an employability development tool is the objective of this report. Toward this end a discussion of the issues which create a need for work experience, the advantages of the work experience approach and the evolution of work experience models developed under categorial programs is undertaken. Based on this background, the key elements of successful work experience program models are isolated and examined in detail. The authors hope that this will lead to new possibilities for creative and flexible programming and a greater appreciation of the range of activities which occur under the category "work experience."

181. Policy Research Section, Florida Office of Manpower Planning. <u>On Site Visits to Florida Prime Sponsors</u>. Tallahassee, Florida: Policy Research Section, Florida Office of Manpower Planning, 1976.

A review of prime sponsors' activities in the state of Florida in terms of an assessment of the area's population and economy, identification of employment and income needs, planned program activities, program and agency linkages, program performance, delivery mechanism, decision-making process and the advisory council.

182. Positive Futures, Inc. <u>Final Report on Prime Sponsor Utilization of Colleges and Universities in the Implementation of CETA Youth Programs</u>. Washington, D.C.: Employment and Training Administration, 1979. L37.2: C68

The provision of a reliable data base on the nature and extent to which CETA prime sponsors utilize both black and non-black colleges and universities to facilitate implementation of Title III (new Title IV) youth program initiatives is the purpose of this report. The study surveys black colleges and universities to determine youth training/ employment capabilities, knowledge of CETA, and the extent of program linkages with Department of Labor and/or prime sponsors. Similar data are obtained for a small sample of non-minority colleges.

183. Prentice, Dinah (editor). <u>CETA/YEDPA Education Policy</u>. Washington, D. C.: National Association of State Boards of Education, 1979.

The work of a national task force on youth employment policy, convened to identify and address the basic educational issues generated by the Youth Employment and Demonstration Projects Act (YEDPA) which is part of the Comprehensive Employment and Training Act (CETA), is discussed. Major topics are: (1) educational credit for work experience; (2) governance issues; (3) career guidance and counseling; (4) program development for special populations; (5) school facilities, personnel, and Public Service Employment; and (6) private sector, manpower, and education agencies. Priorities are assigned to the issues raised. Recommendations can be summarized as a need for collaboration at all levels, among education, employment, and training agencies; program assessment and identification of exemplary programs; and technical assistance to both existing and potential programs. (ERIC)

184. Pressley, Calvin and James McGraw. Classroom Training – The OIC Approach: CETA Program Models. Washington, D.C.: Employment & Training Administration, 1978. L37.8/6: C56

This monograph provides useful information to assist those persons responsible for classroom training as a basic component of employment and training programs. It evaluates the advantages and disadvantages of classroom training in the light of the underlying philosophy and experience of the Opportunities Industrialization Centers (OIC) which attempt to reach their 'economically disadvantaged' clientele by extending efforts beyond teaching occupational skills. According to the authors, the relevance of training to the enrollees and the community is a basic requirement and industrial involvement is essential. The important ingredients of successful classroom training are identified. They include programs which are client-centered; provide individualized instruction; provide employment-related counseling; and include team training and assessment. In addition, the profile of successful classroom training consists of a training environment in which a real work setting is simulated in the classroom with the program being delivered on an individualized basis by experienced practitioners as instructors. Finally, the authors offer a number of criteria for evaluating the effectiveness of classroom training.

185. Reder, Melvin W. Dual Aspect Jobs. Washington, D.C.: National Commission for Manpower Policy, 1978. Y3.M 31: 9/21

An analysis of PSE jobs reveals that they are unsatisfactory in terms of efficiency, are deadend, and are low paying. Hence, a new instrument for manpower policy is proposed. This is the "Dual Aspect Jobs," (DAJ) designed to have the government attract large corporations to provide "sustainable" jobs in the economy. The jobs have a dual aspect: regular productive activity and socially needed services. Such an expansion would be based on government subsidies to the firms in the form of government contracts. (ERIC)

186. Reid, Clifford E. Some Evidence on the Effect of Manpower Training Programs on The Black/White Wage Differential. Washington, D.C.: U.S. Department of Labor, 1974. NTIS PB283140/AS

This study presents a simple method for estimating one aspect of the distributional effect of employment and training programs. In particular, the effect of training programs on the average wage of black workers relative to the average wage of white workers is examined. It appears to depend on three factors: (1) the proportion of the labor forces that have undergone training; (2) the extent to which training increases the wages of black workers relative to white workers; and (3) the difference in the effects of the presence of training programs on the wages of black and white workers who have not undergone training. The sex and racial composition of trainees is also examined.

It is concluded that although the effect of training programs on the black/white wage differential was positive and had steadily increased since 1963, the estimates are very small. Black females are the recipients of most of the redistributional benefits of training programs. In 1972 the black/white ratio for men was 0.5 percent greater than it would have been in the absence of training programs, while for females the ratio was 1.4 percent greater than it would have been in the absence of such programs. It is further concluded that the institutional training program has had little impact on the redistribution of income from whites to blacks. For males the difference between having training programs and not having them ranges from .001 to .003, and for females the range is from .001 to .013. (ASPER)

187. Reid, Clifford E. "Some Evidence on the Effect of Manpower Programs on the Black/White Wage Differential," Journal of Human Resources, 11, Summer, 1976, pp. 402-410.

This paper develops a method for estimating one aspect of the distributional effect of employment and training programs. Using data from Manpower Development and Training Act programs, the impact on the average wage of black workers relative to the impact on the average wage of white workers is examined. The impacts are divided into enrollment, training, and displacement effects. The results suggest a positive and increasing impact on the black/white wage ratio although the impact is very small.

188. Reischauer, Robert D. "The Economy, the Federal Budget, and Prospects for Urban Aid," in Roy Bahl (editor). The Fiscal Outlook for Cities. Syracuse, New York: Syracuse University Press, 1978.

In a study focusing on the impacts of inflation and recession on federal aid to cities, the author concludes that over the long-run, the prospects for increased urban aid will probably continue to depend more upon economic development and constraints placed on the federal budget than upon initiatives such as the Carter administration's "New Partnership." In particular, he reviews the impacts of CETA public service employment and concludes that during the first nine months of the 1977-78 CETA buildup, rough data indicate a 42 percent substitution rate. These crude data suggest the persistence of the historic tendency of state and local governments to slow down their own hiring when federally supported PSE slots are available, according to the author.

189. Reyes, (J.A.) Associates, Inc. The Public Employment Program: An Impact Assessment, Volume I. Washington, D.C.: J. A. Reyes Associates, Inc., 1974.

Volume I contains the findings and a comprehensive analysis of a study designed to determine the ways in which subsidized public employment impacted upon State and local institutions, in particular: (1) were new jobs created; (2) were public services improved or increased; and (3) was there a change in the characteristics of public employees. Included as part of this volume is a discussion of the early phases of the transition of the Public employees. Also as part of this volume is a discussion of the early phases of the transition of the Public Employment Program (PEP) to the Comprehensive Employment and Training Program (CETA). The volume also contains a precis of the final report, as well as appendices which include all of the interview guides, and supplemental data relating to information contained in the main section of the report. (NTIS)

190. Reyes, (J. A.) Associates, Inc. The Public Employment Program: An Impact Assessment, Volume II. Site Reports. Washington, D.C.: J. A. Reyes Associates, Inc., 1974.

Volume II contains a site report for each of the 20 sample localities visited during the course of the study designed to determine whether and to what extent Public Employment Program (PEP) funding affected: (1) job creation and/or restructuring; (2) the characteristics of the public work force; and (3) the quantity and quality of municipal services. The highlights of program operations at each site are reviewed. (NTIS)

191. Ripley, Randall B. and Associates. Areawide Planning in CETA. Washington, D.C.: Employment and Training Administration, 1979. L37.14: 74

A study of planning by prime sponsor staff for old Title I (new Title II A, B and C) of CETA was undertaken with data from twelve prime sponsors. The intensive field work done in these twelve was combined with national data and data from thirty prime sponsors studied by previous projects to isolate those factors which contribute to improving program performance. The results suggest that careful planning can improve program performance. But, planning is only one of many aspects of management which must be handled well if improvement is to be made. Most of these other factors are manipulatable at the local level, and those that are not do not create severe constraints on what can be achieved. In reaching these conclusions three planning models were identified, contextual factors were analyzed, program performance was measured, and exemplary approaches to critical elements of planning were identified.

192. Ripley, Randall B. CETA Prime Sponsor Management Decisions and Programs Goal Achievement. Washinton, D.C.: U.S. Department of Labor, 1977. L37.14: 56

Data were collected from fifteen prime sponsors in each of the ten Department of Labor regions, plus the seventeen prime sponsors covered in an earlier report for the state of Ohio. It reveals that program decisions were mostly affected by factors controlled considerably by local prime sponsors; for example, program mix and sub-contracting, (rather than the level of unemployment and the demographic composition of the community), specific recommendations to improve prime sponsor's activities are presented. The research evaluates Titles I, II, and VI in terms of program design, participants, and performance. (ERIC)

193. Ripley, Randall B. The Implementation of CETA in Ohio. Columbus, Ohio: Ohio State University Press, 1977.

This work is the last of a series of reports on the implementation of the Comprehensive Employment and Training Act (CETA) in Ohio from the inception of the program in 1974 through mid 1976. It compares 16 of the 17 prime sponsors in the State. The monograph describes and explains patterns of influence over decision making at local levels, a variety of programmatic choices, and patterns of client usage and services. Comments are made on the roles of the state and the Chicago regional office of the Department of Labor with regard to Ohio prime sponsors. The authors conclude that there are three main problems and three main principal achievements of CETA in Ohio. The problems relate to decreased or low level services to the most disadvantaged of eligible CETA clients, less attention to training and work experience programs, and a vague and shifting federal role in CETA. The principal achievements discussed are innovative and seemingly successful programs developed by some prime sponsors in the face of political and economic pressures, growing professionalism of the CETA system, and some meaningful and influential involvement in CETA decision making through manpower planning councils. Recommendations are made concerning client service patterns, program comprehensiveness, PSE, Manpower Planning Councils, the regional office of DOL, and the state. The report contains charts illustrating models of CETA implementation and a bibliography. (ERIC)

194. Rosen, Howard. Recent Manpower Legislation and Programs: Implications for Research and Development. Columbus, Ohio: Ohio State University Press, 1975.

Recent economic trends are linked with manpower legislation and the establishment of various programs: the Manpower Development and Training Act of 1962, the Comprehensive Employment and Training Act of 1973, and the Emergency Jobs and Employment Assistance Act of 1974. These legislative acts opened public service jobs and established federal programs for special unemployment assistance. The role of these manpower programs in alleviating the unemployment situation and the need to develop human resources to meet employment needs in the future are discussed. Comprehensive manpower plans and the establishment of planning councils are reviewed. Suggestions for major efforts under manpower programs include: special programs for disadvantaged clients, providing income assistance to ex-offenders, placing trained minority women in jobs commensurate with their skills, and improving the employment service. Other areas for research and development, such as the transition from school to work for young people, and the increasing unemployment rate for black teenagers, are mentioned. (ERIC)

195. Rosen, Summer M. "CETA: Some Case Studies," Social Policy, 6, November/December, 1975, pp. 44-48.

Characteristics of health institutions which influence their inter-actions with Public Service Employment programs and problems of interagency coordination are considered in this study. Specific findings of site visits where health personnel are enrolled in the Comprehensive Employment and Training Act (CETA) are discussed. (ERIC)

196. Sawhney, Pawan K., Robert H. Jantzen, and Irwin L. Herrnstadt, "The Differential Impact of CETA Training," Industrial and Labor Relations Review, 35, January, 1982, pp. 243-51.

This study analyzes the effectiveness of CETA skill training programs in Boston, using three techniques not often employed in such evaluation studies--a comparison group, multiple regressions incorporating an unusually large number of explanatory variables, and an examination of the effects of differences in the type of skill-training provided. The authors find that these programs provided participants with significant wage and employment bene-fits, particularly when participants obtained jobs on which they could use the skills they learned. The results also showed, however, that the stability of postprogram employment is sensitive to the type of training received and postprogram wages are even more so. (ILRR)

197. Sawyer, James. "Lessons for Prime Sponsors." Manpower, April, 1974. pp. 16-24.

Characteristics of successful local manpower training are identi-fied in this article and a list of success factors such as staff services and efforts at cooperation is provided.

198. Schapiro, E. "Wage Inflation, Manpower Training and the Phillips Curve: A Graphic Integration," American Economist, 25, Spring, 1981, pp. 17-21.

The short run unemployment-inflation trade-off can be improved by manpower training, i.e. the Phillips curve could be shifted to the left by providing the untrained, unemployed with minimum skills to qualify for entry-level jobs. The increased supply of qualified entrants would decrease the overall unemployment rate and retard the rate of wage inflation by lessening the upward pressure in money wages by those workers previously employed at lower level positions. Increases in expenditures for training programs will make this possible. This work traces the effect of such action and isolates the factors which influence the strength of the responses (e.g. type of training, objective of training . . .).

199. Schiller, Bradley R. "Lessons from WIN: A Manpower Evaluation," Journal of Human Resources, 13, Fall, 1978, pp. 502-23.

The Work Incentive (WIN) program provides employment, training, and supportive services to welfare recipients. In this paper, the WIN program is evaluated on the basis of: 1) its average net impact on participant earnings and welfare dependency, 2) its relative impact on providing specific services (e.g., OJT, classroom training) to participants with varying work histories, and 3) its average and relative cost effectiveness. It is concluded that WIN has been very effective in serving welfare recipients who have poor work histories despite the modest average gain observed for the program as a whole; subsidized public employment is singled out as a particularly effective tool for increasing the employment and earnings of welfare recipients. (JHR)

200. Schroeder, Larry D. and Others. Income Distribution Effects of Manpower Programs. Washington, D.C.: U.S. Department of Labor, 1975. NTIS PB257074/AS

Because of the lack of methodology for equity analysis, this study was limited to a review of existing material in public finance for analyzing the implications of studies of income distributional effects of employment and training programs. The evidence suggests that higher income participants benefit more than lower level participants, and that program benefits are maldistributed among the States.

Next, estimates of short-run impacts of employment and training programs were made by constructing a two-skill level, three-sector theoretical equilibrium economic model, which shows that the programs' transformation of a lower skill level of labor into a higher skill level alters the distribution of income, with trainees benefiting relative to nontrained cohorts, while owners of capital find their returns on all labor increasing. In addition, both stochastic and behavioral models of intergenerational income distribution and population mobility are considered, showing that a combination of both methodological approaches should lead to improved intergenerational models. (ASPER)

201. Schroeder, Larry D., David L. Sjoquist and Paula E. Stephan, "The Allocation of Employment and Training Funds Across States," Policy Analysis, 6, Fall, 1980, pp. 395-407.

The allocation of employment and training program grants differs among states. A state's "fair share" can be explained in terms of funding formulas and funding process. This research examines the equity of the allocation of funds in terms of program objectives, factors in the funding formulas, and the need for local initiative. The findings suggest that the obligation procedure plays a key role in accounting for the substantial variations that exist in funding among states.

202. Sheppard, Harold L. The Nature of the Job Problem and the Role of New Public Service Employment. Kalamazoo, Michigan: W. E. Upjohn Institute for Employment Research, 1969.

Intended to promote discussion about unemployment and underemployment in America, this report considers the question of who among the poor do, or do not work, and why; the occupations, industries, regional distribution, and other characteristics of the working poor; estimates as to how many more jobs could be filled or created during 1965-75; and the role of private and public employers in meeting "hard core" employment needs. Finally, the report asserts the need to combine current training and hiring efforts in the private sector with the expansion and provision of Public Service Employment at various levels of government and in nonprofit organizations. (ERIC)

203. Simeral, Margaret H. "The Impact of the Public Employment Program on Sex-Related Wage Differentials," Industrial and Labor Relations Review, 31, July, 1978, pp. 509-519.

In this paper Margaret Simeral examines the source of the sexual wage differential among a group of participants in the Economic Impact Project of the Public Employment Program of 1971 and examines the impact of the program on that differential. The paper concludes that a public service program such as PEP could be an effective part of a short-term public policy to alleviate sexual inequalities in the labor market. Such a program has the potential of affecting the wage differential by redistributing job opportunities, by decreasing the magnitude of interoccupational wage differentials, and by enhancing the productivity of participants by providing on-the-job training and experience. The pre-PEP wage differential was found to result from the sexual occupational distribution and the worker-trait requirements of men's and women's jobs. Although a PEP type program can effectively correct these inequalities, it does so only temporarily. The analysis of post-PEP jobs showed that wage differential reverted to its pre-PEP level. The fact that such gains may not be transferred to the post-policy period casts serious doubts on the ability of a temporary public service employment program to improve the status of women over the long run.

204. Smith, Ralph E. "The Opportunity Cost of Participation in a Training Program," Journal of Human Resources, 6, Fall, 1971, pp. 510-519.

An analytical model for estimating the earnings foregone by participants in employment and training programs is developed in this paper and tested using data from Manpower Development and Training Act institutional training programs. The results suggest that the opportunity costs are large and important. They raise the issues of the potential loss to the economy as the result of such programs and the redistributional impacts of such programs.

205. Smith, Robert S. and Hugh M. Pitcher. The Neighborhood Youth Corps: An Impact Evaluation. Washington, D.C.: U.S. Department of Labor, 1973. NTIS PB268605/AS

This study attempts to evaluate the success of the Neighborhood Youth Corps (NYC) in attaining four goals: (1) redistributing income to the poor; (2) increasing employment opportunities for teenagers; (3) reducing teenage crime rates; and (4) increasing the lifetime earnings of participants through job experience and encouragement to stay in school.

It is found that the NYC program was essentially redistributive; income was transferred from middle- and upper-income groups to the poor. The summer program appears to be slightly more redistributive than the in-school program, at least in the short-run. Evidence on the employment effect of NYC is not conclusive nor credible, and requested data were lacking for evaluation of changes in teenage employment that may stem from NYC. The effects of NYC on teenage crime rates are essentially unknown and, with available data, unknowable. Evidence on the long-run impact of NYC on earnings is likewise unconvincing; estimates alternate between rates of return that are inordinately high and zero. Evidence with respect to educational attainment is likewise conflicting. It is, therefore, concluded that the long-run effects of NYC are unknown, because better data are needed. (ASPER)

206. Snedeker, Bonnie B. and David M. Snedeker. CETA: Decentralization on Trial. Salt Lake City, Utah: Olympus Press, 1978.

The objective of the authors is "to judge the effectiveness of CETA." Their judgement is based on information gathered in interviews with individuals involved with CETA at all levels of government. The book capsulizes pre-CETA manpower policy and focuses on the changes in policy brought about by CETA with its goals of decentralization, decategorization and consolidation. Special attention is given to changes in methods of needs assessment, program planning and development, service development, and program management, monitoring and evaluation. The PSE responsibilities created by CETA Title VI are studied. The book concludes with a summary of the current issues and the outlook for the future.

207. Somers, Gerald G. and Ernst W. Stromsdorfer. "A Cost-Effectiveness Analysis of In-School and Summer Neighborhood Youth Corps: A Nationwide Evaluation," in David Nachmias (editor). The Practice of Policy Evaluation. New York, New York: St. Martin's Press, 1980, pp. 67-80.

The report analyzes the extent to which the in-school and summer NYC has succeeded in achieving the objectives legislated for it by Congress. This evaluation is conducted by the use of multiple-regression techniques and cost-effectiveness analysis to investigate the costs and benefits of the program. Costs and benefits are estimated in private terms, for society, and for the federal government. The data for measurement of costs and benefits are gained from government records, a field questionnaire, and school record data sheets.

208. Stafford, Frank P. A Decision Theoretic Approach to the Evaluation of Manpower Programs. Washington, D.C.: U.S. Department of Labor, 1975. NTIS PB256256/AS

This paper outlines a method for determining sample size for program evaluation in a cost/benefit framework.

The main point is that, given a prior distribution on the outcome
parameter of the policy, a sample size can be chosen such that the
marginal expected gain from additional sampling equals the marginal
cost of sampling. This will, in general, differ from the criteria
of "significant at the 5-percent or 1-percent level." Programs that
are more economically important should generally be subjected to
greater sampling. In programs which, prior to sampling, are viewed
as close to breakeven values, there should be a monotonically
increasing Expected Value of Sample Information (EVSI) as sample
size grows. The problems posed by sequential sampling are of
considerable practical importance as well, but formal treatment requires a complex analysis not provided here. (ASPER)

209. Stanfield, Robert E. The Uses of Paraprofessionals in the Delivery
of Manpower and Social Services Through Public Service Employment: The
Vermont Experience. Montpelier, Vermont: Vermont State Employment
Service, 1973. NTIS TB231897/0GI

Trainees in a Public Service Employment program may find jobs as
paraprofessional aides in manpower agencies, social services, and
human services. The work experience is valuable for the trainees;
however, the actual structure of their training needs careful
attention: supervisors are likely to rate the effectiveness of
on-the-job training highly, while trainees give at least equal
credit to the "common sense" which they bring to the job. Also,
there may be little consistency in the training experience of
different trainees. One answer to this problem is for employers to
be more flexible in accepting the practical experience and "common
sense" of the trainees as a substitute for more formal requirements
while at the same time formalizing the necessary on-the-job training into a regular curriculum. Transferability and placement
prospects for trainees in paraprofessional slots are limited,
especially in view of the tight job market. (ERIC)

210. Stephan, Paula E. The Determinants of Training Produced in the
Private Sector. Washington, D.C.: U.S. Department of Labor, 1974.
NTIS PB256666/AS

This study examines the behavioral determinants of the private
sector's demand for training subsequent to formal education, to
determine whether Government employment and training programs
provide primary or secondary benefits. A human capital investment
model is used to analyze the determinants of the quantity of human
capital that would be acquired by the individual at a given time in
the absence of a Government program. The dampening effect on
training of discrimination, myopic behavior, imperfect access to
the capital market, unemployment, and minimum wage legislation is
discussed.

It is found that the Government could indirectly stimulate the
training that individuals produce by providing better information
flows, by helping to eliminate the negative economic effects of
discrimination, by relaxing the minimum wage legislation for young
people, and by providing some access to the capital market for
human capital needs. As for the Government's entering the training
business, there was some evidence that benefits produced by pro-

grams such as the Manpower Development and Training Act (MDTA) may be only temporary. (ASPER)

211. Sum, Andrew, Katherine Mazzeo, Francis McLaughlin, and Jeffrey Zornitsky. Evaluating the Performance of Employment and Training Programs at the Local Level, Volumes 1-4. Washington, D.C.: Department of Labor, 1978.

The first volume provides an overview of the role of program evaluation in the planning, design and administration of employment and training programs at the local level. It also contains a description and assessment of the evaluation activities of New England prime sponsors since 1975.

The second volume presents a detailed discussion and analysis of the interrelationships between the planning, monitoring and evaluation functions. Three separate chapters are devoted to a detailed description and analysis, as well as specific application of process, outcome and benefit-cost evaluation methodologies.

Volume three focuses upon a series of issues related to the design and implementation of follow-up studies at the local prime sponsor level. The experience of the city of Boston prime sponsor in conducting follow-up studies of Title I program terminees and in analyzing the data obtained through such studies are documented in detail. The findings of these follow-up studies are then reviewed and analyzed, and their implications for future program planning are discussed. The extention of this follow-up system throughout the state of Massachusetts is highlighted in the final chapter of this volume. It also contains a technical supplement designed to acquaint prime sponsor planning and evaluation staffs with a number of statistical techniques that can be utilized in analyzing the findings of follow-up studies.

Volume four contains the following: (1) a summary of the key issues and findings contained in each volume and (2) the table of contents for each volume.

212. Taggart, Robert. A Fisherman's Guide: An Assessment of Training and Remediation Strategies. Kalamazoo, Michigan: W. E. Upjohn Institute for Employment Research, 1981.

The great wealth of research results concerning employment and training programs is synthesized and analyzed in this work. The author concludes from this assessment that improvement in existing programs (CETA) should be made gradually with a realignment of program directions combined with new training activites and guidelines. In his view, training should receive top priority in order that those individuals who are unemployed and underemployed can be equipped to meet future labor requirements of business and industry in a period in which the U.S. economy is entering a situation of potential labor shortage.

In order that the new aims of employment and training programs are met, some long accepted tenents of policy must be changed, according to Taggart. Income maintenance should be deemphasized. In its place a federally mandated competency system should be developed. This system would measure academic and vocational skill acquisition; organize individualized, self-paced instruction; judge the effectiveness of training institutions; and certify competencies attained. In addition, training for the disadvantaged should utilize mainstream institutions wherever possible, and long-term training should be encouraged by set-asides and incentive grants. Finally, although national impact studies indicate substantial benefit differences among programs, prime sponsors, who cannot undertake long-term follow-ups with comparison groups and focus instead on short-term outcome including in-program gains by participants, do not always see such differences. Yet they do see that regardless of program the most important determinant of gains is length of time in program.

Thus, Taggart reduces his study to some simple conclusions: CETA (or its successor) should place more emphasis on training; duration of stay in program should be longer; and on-the-job training opportunities should be expanded. In addition, placement efforts should go hand-in-hand with training with the emphasis on securing training related jobs. Competency attainment should be stressed, performance standards maintained, and career opportunities made available for those who prove themselves in the system.

213. Taggart, Robert, (editor). <u>Job Creation: What Works?</u> Salt Lake City, Utah: Olympus Press, 1977.

This book is a collection of five papers, each of which examines one of the tools of job creation and stimulus: tax cuts, wage subsidies, reduced worktime, public works and public service employment. The purpose is not just to summarize the experience with each of the tools, but to reach an understanding of their relative effectiveness and their role in a coordinated national manpower policy. Each of the papers is followed by a condensed text of the comments and discussion of the topic by the members of the National Council on Employment Policy, before whom the papers were presented at Michigan State University in 1977.

214. Taggart, Robert. <u>Summer Program for Economically Disadvantaged Youth (SPEDY)</u>. Washington, D.C.: Employment and Training Administration, 1978. L37.2: Su61978

Four papers providing information on the Summer Program for Economically Disadvantaged Youth (SPEDY) are contained in this monograph. They are written by practitioners involved with the program at the local level and suggest ways of improving the program. Each paper focuses on the basic design and operational mechanics of the program in a particular area. The areas are Tacoma, Washington; Balance-of-State, Texas; Richmond, Virginia; and various Minnesota sites. The areas were chosen because of their solid programs.

215. Toews, Curtis, et al. <u>Rural Jobs from Rural Public Works: A Rural Employment Outreach Experimental and Demonstration Project, Phase Two, February 1, 1977 to January 31, 1978</u>. Washington, D.C.: The National Rural Center, 1978.

This report describes the continued activities and research inferences of the second year of an experimental and demonstration
project designed to increase the number of local, minority and/or
economically disadvantaged persons employed on federally-financed
construction projects in rural areas. Second year activities
centered on the Tennessee-Tombigbee Waterway Project in Alabama and
Mississippi, the Red River Waterway Project in Louisiana, The
Ouachita-Black River Waterway Project in Arkansas and Louisiana,
the Richard B. Russell Dam Project in Georgia and South Carolina,
and the Choke Canyon Dam in Texas. Affirmative action programs
were established for each area and actions for the implementation
of programs for the recruitment and training for employment of
minority and/or economically disadvantaged persons were instituted.
Research into the efficacy of special training programs implemented
for construction employment on the Waterway was performed. (NTIS)

216. Turner, Susan and Carolyn Conradus. Supportive Services: CETA
Program Models. Washington, D.C.: Employment and Training Administration, 1978. L37.8/6: Su7

This report reviews the experience of categorical programs in
developing and providing supportive services to improve client
employability. Supportive services include counseling, program and
employment orientation, educational services, transportation, child
care, physical and mental health services, legal and bonding
services, and use of petty cash funds. The review concludes that
supportive services should be provided only if they lead to employment. To assist program planners the report identifies selected
elements of the process and describes four models for the delivery
of supportive services.

217. Ulman, Lloyd (editor). Manpower Programs in the Policy Mix.
Baltimore, Maryland: Johns Hopkins University Press, 1973.

This book contains five articles aimed at providing a better understanding of the role of employment and training programs in public
policy. The first is R. A. Gordon's "Some Macroeconomic Aspects of
Manpower Policy." Gordon considers the extent to which employment
and training can contribute to solving the full employment-price
stability issue. This topic continues in the second paper by
Charles C. Holt and others entitled "Manpower Policies to Reduce
Inflation and Unemployment." The third paper by Lester C. Thurow
considers the redistributional impacts of employment and training
programs while Sar A. Levitan considers the structure of programs
and their possible impacts in the fourth paper entitled "Manpower
Programs for a Healthier Economy." The final paper by Rudolf
Meider and Rolf Andersson is "The Overall Impact of an Active Labor
Market Policy in Sweden." This considers the Swedish use of labor
market policy to ease the compatibility of full employment and
economic stability goals.

218. Ulmer, Melville J. "Toward Public Employment and Economic Stability," Journal of Economic Issues, 6, December, 1972, pp. 149-170.

In this article Ulmer states that poverty and unemployment can be
best combatted through an expansive public employment program. The

author argues that this program will not be inflationary if it is completely financed through taxes. The taxes would ensure that overall spending in the private sector would not rise above its prevailing noninflationary level. Simultaneously, private sector production and output would be expanded, utilizing otherwise idle labor for the purpose of satisfying the country's most urgent social needs.

219. U.S. Congress. Comprehensive Employment and Training Act Amendments of 1978. Conference Report (To accompany S.2570). 95th Congress, 2nd Session, 1978. 95-2: H.rp. 1124

This conference report covers the 1978 ammendments to the Comprehensive and Employment Training Act. The first two-thirds of the report reviews each of the eight titles comprising the amendments. The last third of the report notes the differences between the Senate bill and the House amendment and the substitute agreed to in conference. (CIS)

220. U.S. Congress', House of Representatives, Committee on Education and Labor. Compilation of Selected Federal Legislation Relating to Employment and Training. 96th Congress, 1st Session, 1979. Y4.Ed 8/1: L52/17

This work is a compilation of fourteen federal laws covering employment and training. These are as follow: (1) Comprehensive Employment and Training Act of 1973, as amended; (2) Full Employment and Balanced Growth Act of 1978 (Humphrey-Hawkins Act); (3) National Apprenticeship Act; (4) Reimbursement for Unemployment Benefits Paid on Basis of Public Service Employment (Title II, Part B, Emergency Jobs and Unemployment Assistance Act of 1974); (5) Wagner-Peyser Act; (6) Work Incentive Program (Title IV, Social Security Act); (7) WIN Tax Credits, Targeted Job Tax Credit; (8) Youth Conservation Corps Act of 1970; (9) Employment Opportunities for Handicapped Individuals Act; (10) excerpts from the Economic Opportunity Act of 1964; (11) Older Americans Community Service Employment Act; (12) Youth Employment (Title III, Part F. Elementary and Secondary Act of 1965); (13) Work Study Programs (Title IV, Part C, Higher Education Act of 1965); and (14) the Vocational Education Act of 1963. (ERIC)

221. U.S. Department of Labor. Assessing Large Scale Public Job Creation. Washington, D.C.: GPO, 1979. L37.14:67

Job creation in the public sector has played an increasingly important role in recent years. The purpose of this study is to assess the feasibility of large-scale countercyclical job creation activities by considering numbers, characteristics, costs, and meaningfulness of work. Moreover, administrative and operational problems of implementing and phasing out PSE projects are analyzed.

222. U.S. Department of Labor. Conference Report on Evaluating the 1977 Economic Stimulus Package. Washington, D.C.: GPO, 1978. L1.2: Ec7/3

This report includes five papers presented at a 1977 conference held at the Brookings Institution to consider how to evaluate the performance of four of the five components of the President's 1977 Economic Stimulus Appropriations Act.

The papers do not provide program evaluations, rather, the authors were requested to assess the adequacy of existing evaluation plans and to recommend changes in methodology.

"Evaluating the Effects of the Employment Tax Credit" by Orley Ashenfelter sets out in a simplified form the accounting details of how the employment tax credit is designed to operate in terms of the change in the wage rate it may be expected to induce. The resulting microeconomic behavioral changes are discussed as well as the macroeconomic issues that must be considered for proper evaluation.

"Approaches to Evaluating the Local Public Works Program" by Jeffrey M. Perloff suggests three econometric studies to analyze and evaluate local public works programs and presents arguments for and against the public works program as a countercyclical policy.

"Evaluating Antirecession Fiscal Assistance" by Edward M. Gramlich examines the existing methods of evaluating the fund allocation mechanisms for fiscal assistance to State and local governments and suggests a broader range of questions to be asked about the program and new ways to conduct an evaluation study of fiscal assistance programs.

"Evaluating the CETA Public Service Employment Program" by Michael Wiseman summarizes the Department of Labor's evaluation for CETA public service employment programs. It distinguishes between evaluation aimed at verifying assumptions upon which public service employment is based, and evaluation aimed at improving the congruence between what public service employment programs are, and what theoretically they should be.

"Evaluating the 1977 Stimulus Package: A Summary Statement" by Michael L. Wachter discusses the problems of overall evaluation. The lack of adequate data--caused by noncomparability of data collected by different Departments--is one of the major problems of evaluation. A number of new sources of data bases are suggested. The author recommends that evaluation studies pay closer attention to the potential tradeoff between short-run demand multipliers and inflation effects. (ASPER)

223. U.S. Department of Labor. Guidelines for the Development of Labor Market Information Needed for CETA Planning Purposes. Washington, D.C.: Employment and Training Administration, 1979. L37.8: M 34/2

The 1978 CETA reauthorization required several types of labor market information not previously required. Because of problems encountered by prime sponsors in meeting these requirements, specific guidelines for the preparation of the needed planning information were established. This work focuses on those data requirements of the eight planning tables specified in the Forms

Preparation Handbook and isolate problems encountered in identifying data sources and/or estimating procedures used.

224. U.S. Department of Labor.   Improving Services to Young Parents
through CETA. Washington, D.C.: GPO, 1980. L37.2: C73/4

The Comprehensive Employment and Training Act has emphasized
services to young people with approximately two-thirds of those
entering CETA in fiscal 1978 and 1979 being under the age of 22.
In this group young parents, both male and female, married and
unmarried, face particular problems. This report is designed to
familiarize prime sponsors with the issues concerning adolescent
pregnancy and parenthood, highlight innovative approaches in
working with young parents, and offer suggestions on how to reach
and serve young parents with CETA.

225. U.S. Department of Labor.   Labor Market Information and CETA
Planning Workshop. Washington, D.C.: GPO, 1978. L37.8. M34

This report outlines and presents the materials used in a course
designed for individuals directly involved in the CETA planning
process at the prime sponsor level and for ETA regional staff
responsible for assessing prime sponsor performance. The ten units
which make up the course are: Employment Program Planning; Problems of Economic Instability; Labor Market Structures; Labor Market
Information; Geography of Labor Markets; Identification of Population Groups in Need of Employment Program Service; Assessing Job
Opportunities; Analyzing the Structure of Employment; Priorities,
Goals, Objectives, and Operational Planning; and an Employment
Program Case Study. The course is designed to develop technical
proficiency in CETA program planning and evoke an appreciation of
the need for a dynamic, continuous planning effort.

226. U.S. Department of Labor. Private Sector Initiative Program: The
PIC is the Keystone. Washington, D.C.: GPO, 1980. L37.2:P93

An explanation of the Private Industry Council (PIC) as part of the
Private Sector Initiative Program is provided in this brief pamphlet. It outlines the goals and objectives of PICs and cites
examples of programs in seven areas. A list of benefits to
employers from the program is provided.

227. U.S. Department of Labor. Survey of Public Employment Program
Terminations, prepared by Automated Services, Inc. Washington, D.C.:
Manpower Administration, July 1973. PB-222 660/3

This study examines public employment program terminations in order
to find out why participants left the program and determines the
post-PEP labor-force status of terminees. Neither question had
been adequately answered by information contained in the national
PEP data file. A nationwide survey of ten urban PEP projects
during November and December of 1972 questioned program terminees
and project administrators. (NTIS)

228. U.S. Department of Labor, Employment and Training Administration. CETA Title VI Project Description Reports, Vol. II. Washington, D.C.: GPO, 1978. L37.2: C73/2

See Abstract under Autry, George (#8).

229. U.S. Department of Labor, Employment and Training Administration. Comprehensive Employment and Training Act: Review and Oversight. Washington, D.C.: GPO, 1975.

This report reviews the establishment and early performance of the comprehensive manpower system established by the Comprehensive Employment and Training Act (CETA). The report is divided into two major sections. Part 1 examines the background and first year results of the CETA program. The legislative and programmatic antecedents to CETA are sketched for the years 1961 to 1973. Program results are then identified from initial implementation and the first year of operation under the following headings: Implementation, Planning Councils, Service Deliverers, Distribution of Resources among Program Activities, Participant Characteristics, and Outcomes. Part 2 discusses major public policy issues revealed from experience to date and presents those issues in four sections. Section 1 on the focus of employment and training programs discusses the population to be served, skill shortages, integration of manpower development and economic development, CETA and categorical programs, public service employment, and CETA and national economic policy. Section 2 discusses CETA prime sponsor relationship to the vocational education and rehabilitation to CETA, strengthening the link between education and work, and defense-oriented manpower services. Section 3 discusses the integration of manpower development programs with income maintenance programs. Section 4 on the development of CETA discusses the scope of operations, the mix of services, local-state-federal roles, and involvement of business and labor in CETA programs. (ERIC)

230. U.S. Department of Labor, Employment and Training Administration. The Implementation of CETA in Eastern Massachusetts and Boston. Washington, D.C.: GPO, 1978. L37.14: 57

The work is a two-part monograph containing reports describing the results of three years of field research on the implementation and impact of CETA in Eastern Massachusetts. The first report, "CETA in Eastern Massachusetts," was prepared by the Alfred P. Sloan School of Management. It describes economic/ employment conditions during 1974-1977 and compares the planning and selection processes, implementation techniques, and overall performance of each prime sponsor. Pre-CETA and post-CETA participnt data is examined for evidence of growth in average wage rates. The paper concludes with future recommendations.

The second report, "The Implementation of CETA in Boston, 1974-1977," was prepared by the Department of Economics, Northeastern University. It examines the Boston manpower system and summarizes its accomplishments under CETA Title I and PSE. The progress of the Boston CETA program toward the goals of decentralization and decategorization of manpower policy is studied. The report concludes by recommending general changes in the CETA program and suggests specific programs for the future.

231. U.S. Department of Labor, Employment and Training Administration. Perspectives on Public Job Creation. Washington, D.C.:   GPO, 1977. L37.14: 52

This is an anthology of papers in which the job creation potential of a major public jobs program is explored from a diversity of viewpoints. The contributing authors were encouraged to adopt a relatively free-wheeling approach to the issue in order to elicit the greatest possible number of ideas, but they were also asked to estimate the employment impact of different approaches to the problem of creating public jobs. The result is the identification of a large number of potential targets for job creation projects in a wide range of occupations and industries which could be extremely useful to prime sponsors seeking ways to implement new programs.

232. U.S. General Accounting Office.   CETA Programs for Disadvantaged Adults -- What Do We Know About Their Enrollees, Services, and Effectiveness? Washington, D.C.:   GAO, 1982. GA1.13:IPE-82-2

This report reviews the four major adult-oriented services provided by CETA and summarizes what is known about enrolles, services and outcomes. The four components analyzed are classroom training, on-the-job training, work experience and public service employment. As a result of its review the GAO found that CETA adult-oriented services were well targeted with enrollees generally being disadvantaged economically, educationally and with regard to employment stability. While outcomes differed for the four services, the differences were expected based on occupational areas covered and participant characteristics. The GAO also found that, on the average, early participants were better off after CETA than before in terms of increased employment and earnings and reduced reliance on public benefits. Finally, because of limited data, CETA's effectiveness can be addressed only in terms of earnings with only a small proportion of the improvement in earnings being attributed directly to CETA. The exceptions are women and participants with extremely poor earnings records prior to CETA entry.

233. U. S. General Accounting Office. More Benefits to Jobless Can Be Attained In Public Service Employment, Prepared by the Comptroller General of the United States. Washington, D.C.:   GAO, 1977. GA1.13: HRD-77-53

This is the third in a series of reports that reviews the Department of Labor's implementation of the Comprehensive Employment and Training Act of 1973. It is reported that public service employment (PSE) programs under CETA provided jobs and other direct benefits to participants and communities. Yet, several problems emerged that lessened the impact of PSE: the availability of limited funding to reduce unemployment; poor targeting (ineligible participants joined the program); and weak transition (relatively few participants obtained permanent, unsubsidized jobs). This report contains many recommendations to the Secretary of Labor and the Congress for improving the program. (NTIS)

234. U.S. General Accounting Office. Information on the Buildup in Public Service Employment. Washington, D.C.: GAO, 1978. GA1.13: HRD-78-57

This report analyzes the effects of the 1976 amendments to Title VI of the Comprehensive Employment and Training Act on long-term unemployed and low-income persons. The following issues were specifically addressed: (1) the ability of the Title VI program to absorb recipients of publicly funded income transfer programs, (2) the extent to which "skimming" of the best qualified, rather than the most needy, takes place, (3) how well the eligibility verification system is working, (4) the impact of financial incentives or disencentives on the decision of income transfer beneficiaries to enter the Title VI program, (5) the types of projects and jobs being created and the capacity to create them, (6) the experience in transitioning Title VI participants into unsubsidized employment, (7) the relationship of various activities involved in the Title VI program, and (8) the extent to which fiscal substitution is taking place.

235. Van Horn, Carl E. "Implementing CETA: The Federal Role". Policy Analysis, 4 Spring, 1978, pp. 159-83.

This article assesses the federal government's role in implementing the first two years of the Comprehensive Employment and Training Act. Following a discussion of CETA and the New Federalism, the study analyzes the impact of the U.S. Department of Labor on major CETA policy issues. Employing a model of intergovernmental policy implementation, Van Horn seeks to account for the nature of federal performance and considers broad implications for the development of intergovernmental policy delivery and federal oversight.

236. Vaughan, Roger J. Public Works as a Countercyclical Device: A Review of the Issues. Santa Monica, California: The Rand Corporation, 1976.

Mr. Vaughan reviews issues relevant to the formulation of a countercyclical public works program. The issues discussed include: the identification of the cyclically unemployed; the measurement of employment cycles; differences among regions and among sectors with respect to cyclical behavior; labor and materials demands of public works projects; methods of financing; and a comparison of public works with other countercyclical instruments. Rand Report Number R-1990-EDA

237. Vernez, George, and Roger Vaughan. Assessment of Countercyclical Public Works and Public Service Employment Programs. Santa Monica, California: The Rand Corporation, 1978.

This report identifies the scope and nature of countercyclical public works and Public Service Employment programs, discusses the characteristics of cyclical unemployment that these programs are designed to alleviate, and examines the effects of these programs on: (1) job creation; (2) speed of job creation; (3) distribution of benefits among regions, industries, occupations, and socio-economic groups; (4) value of public services; (5) program participants; (6) transition from public to private employment; and (7) demand for labor and materials. (NTIS)

238. Werneke, Diane. "Job Creation Programmes: The United States Experience," International Labour Review, 114, July–August, 1976, pp. 43–59.

The United States Job Creation experience is examined. The implications of decentralization, which occurred when CETA superseded the MDTA and EOA in 1973, are discussed, as well as the extent to which the programs have achieved their objectives. Finally, consideration is given to some possible orientations for manpower policy in the future. The author concludes that programs designed to provide jobs for workers unable to find employment when labor markets are functioning efficiently have been unsuccessful. Countercyclical programs were found to be effective but not without problems.

239. Westat, Inc. Continuous Longitudinal Manpower Survey. Follow-up Report No. 1. Post-Program Experience and Pre/Post Comparisons for Terminees Who Entered CETA in January–June 1975. Washington, D. C.: Employment and Training Administration, 1978. L37.2: M31/fol.rp.1

This report is based on interviews of CETA participants conducted approximately 18 months after participants had entered CETA. It presents data on the post-program experience of these participants who were enrolled in Title I, II or IV adult-oriented programs and who had been terminated by the time of the follow-up interview. The sample consists of approximately 320,000 terminees who had been out of the program at least three months and a subgroup of 193,000 who had been terminated for at least one year. Terminees include both program dropouts and program completers. The major findings include: 1) higher post-program levels of employment and earnings of participants despite declining post-program economic conditions, 2) improvements in earnings and employment over time for terminees, and 3) a positive attitude of terminees toward their CETA experience.

240. Westat, Inc. Continuous Longitudinal Manpower Survey. Follow-up Report No. 2. Post-Program Experiences and Pre/Post Comparisons for Terminees Who Entered CETA During Fiscal Year 1976 (July 1975–June 1976). Washington, D. C.: Employment and Training Administration, 1979. L37.2: M31/fol.rp.2

This is the second report based on interviews of CETA participants conducted approximately 18 months after they had entered CETA. It differs from the first follow-up report (see Westat, Inc. CLMS, Follow-up Report No. 1) in that it covers a sample of participants from the whole of fiscal year 1976. Like the first report, it presents data on the post-program experience of those participants who were enrolled in Title I, II or IV adult-oriented programs and who had been terminated by the time of the follow-up interview. The sample consists of approximately 424,000 terminees who had been out of the program at least three months and a subgroup of 251,000 who had been terminated for at least one year. Terminees consisted of both program dropouts and program completers. The major findings include: 1) sharply higher employment and earnings after termination when compared with pre-program experiences, 2) an improvement in post-program employment and earnings over time, 3) important variations depending upon pre-enrollment employment backgrounds and other background characteristics, 4) on-the-job training yielding the largest gain in annualized earnings, and 5) a highly positive rating of CETA by participants.

241. Westat, Inc. Continuous Longitudinal Manpower Survey. Report No. 1-12. Washington, D.C.: Employment and Training Administration, 1976-1981. L37.2: M31/rp.1-12.

These reports describe the persons selected by prime sponsors for the various programs offered under CETA in fiscal years 1975-1979. They provide baseline data for future evaluations of CETA program impacts and a basis for analyzing trends in enrollee characteristics. The reports review CETA during the appropriate fiscal year, discuss new enrollments during the period, and isolate selected characteristics and pre-program labor market experiences of new enrollees.

242. Westat, Inc. Continuous Longitudinal Manpower Survey. The Impact of CETA on Participant Earnings: Working Paper No. 1. Washington, D. C.: Employment and Training Administration, 1980. NTIS PB80-146632

This report presents the first available data concerning the earnings impact of CETA. Data for participants who enrolled during the first two quarters of calendar 1975 were collected as part of the Continuous Longitudinal Manpower Survey (CLMS). This is computed using three different options with information for a comparison group drawn from the Current Population Survey (CPS). The earnings data used come from the Social Security annual earnings records. Although several substantial problems are present such as inter-title transfers of participants not being adequately monitored, the matching of participants and comparison groups with respect to unmeasured characteristics, the lack of coverage of some earnings by Social Security, the possibility of CETA participants being included in the CPS, and the time period chosen representing an abnormally high rate of filling public service employment slots; the study does involve significant methodological advances and important substantive conclusions. While considered highly tentative, the conclusions support a positive contribution to post-program earnings as a result of CETA participation.

243. Westat, Inc. Continuous Longitudinal Manpower Survey. The Impact of CETA on Participant Earnings: Working Paper No. 2. Washington, D.C.: Employment and Training Administration, 1980. NTIS PB81-103467

This paper explores further methodological approaches to the question of estimating the impact of CETA on participant earnings. Using data from the Continuous Longitudinal Manpower Survey (CLMS), it extends the match list options for matching CLMS and Current Population Survey (CPS) files developed in Working Paper No. 1 by stratifying the CLMS and CPS populations into "lower earners" and "higher earners" groups. The paper finds that such a split does increase the precision of the impact estimates, particularly for those with low pre-CETA earnings. The results also indicate that gains are greater for those who have stayed in the program longer, and that there are much higher net earnings gains in postprogram years for those who are placed in employment upon termination than for those who drop out or are not placed.

244. Westat, Inc. Handbook for CLMS Public Use Tapes: January 1975-September 1977 Enrollees. Rockville, Maryland: Westat, 1981.

This handbook is part of the documentation developed for use with the public use tapes derived from the Continuous Longitudinal Manpower Survey (CLMS). It contains general information on CETA and the CLMS and on the contents of the tapes released for public use. The tapes currently available are: CLMS-1 which contains data for 6,650 individuals newly enrolled in CETA between July 1975 and June 1976 (Fiscal Year 1976), and CPS-1 which contains data for 81,323 individuals from the Current Population Survey (CPS). The CLMS data include information from prime sponsor files, interview data including follow-up interviews, and annual earnings while the CPS data consist of CPS interview data and annual earnings records.

245. Westat, Inc. Title VI Tracking Study Final Report. Rockville, Maryland: Westat, 1978.

Details of the operational procedures of program recruitment and identification of Title VI eligible participants for a national tracking study of Title VI participants are presented. Personal interviews were carried out in those agencies responsible for screening, verifying and referring applicants, (namely, CETA prime sponsors, state employment security agencies and Welfare department) as well as with project operators (i.e., community agencies operating projects supported by CETA Title VI non-sustaining funds). Moreover, the research work examined those people who dropped out (or were forced out) of the program (i.e, the "non-served" population). These people were mostly reached through telephone interviews. The immediate employment outcomes of the dropouts were compared to those who obtained jobs through Title VI. (ERIC)

246. Wiseman, Michael. "On Giving a Job: The Implementation and Allocation of Public Service Employment," Paper No. 1 in U.S. Congress, Joint Economic Committee. Achieving the Goals of the Employment Act of 1946 Thirtieth Anniversary Review: Volume I Employment. 93rd Congress, 1975. Y4.Ec7: Em7/14

This paper discusses alternative public employment policies and the problems inherent in the programs funded through CETA. Two types of public employment programs are identified--antipoverty and counter-recession. Public service employment under the Emergency Employment Act of 1971 and under CETA are analyzed and approaches to improving the design of programs so that counter-recessionary policy can be better met without sacrificing emphasis on disadvantages workers are isolated.

247. Wiseman, Michael. "Public Employment as Fiscal Policy." Brookings Papers on Economic Activity, 1, 1976, pp. 67-104.

Public employment policies are thought to be useful complements to other fiscal instruments because outlays on job creation have a desirable time frame; have substantial employment impact; can be pinpointed on areas and persons in need; and have, because of tax effects and transfer savings, only a modest impact on the current budget deficit. These properties are reviewed using data for recent public employment programs. The results, with qualifications, are that employment can be created quickly, that estimates of the rate of substitution of subsidized for nonsubsidized employment have been exaggerated, and that allocation procedures do favor minority workers and areas experiencing substantial unemployment. (ERIC)

248. Wiseman, Michael. Studies in Public Service Employment. Berkeley, California: University of California/Berkeley, Institute of Industrial Relations, 1978.

This report summarizes research on various aspects of the use of subsidized employment in the public sector as a policy instrument. There are three papers. The first, "The Age of Cities, the Employment Effects of Business Cycles, and Public Service Employment," discusses factors which determine the inter-urban distribution of the economic dislocation brought about by recession. The second, "CETA-Subsidized Public Employment in San Francisco," evaluates the operation of the public service employment program in one city. The third, "Evaluating the CETA Public Service Employment Program," discusses the Department of Labor's CETA evaluation apparatus as it existed in 1977. (NTIS)

Directory of Publishers

Abt Associates
55 Wheeler Street
Cambridge, MA 02138

Allanheld, Osmun and Co. Publishers, Inc.
Division of Littlefield, Adams
   and Co.
Biblio Distribution Center
81 Adams Drive
Totowa, NJ 07512

American Enterprise Institute
   for Public Policy Research
1150 17th Street, N.W.
Washington, D.C. 20036

American Journal of Agricultural
   Economics
University of Kentucky
Lexington, Kentucky 40506

Brookings Institution
1775 Massachusetts Ave., N.W.
Washington, D.C. 20036

Bureau of Social Science
   Research, Inc.
1990 N.W. M Street
Washington, D.C. 20036

Congressional Budget Office
2nd and D Streets, N.W.
Washington, D.C. 20515

Congressional Information
   Serivces, Inc. (CIS)
4520 East West Hwy.
Suite 800
Washington, D.C. 20014

Delaware University Press
Delaware University
Newark, Delaware 19711

Employment and Training Admin-
   istration
U.S. Department of Labor
Patrick Henry Bldg, Room 10225
601 D Street, N.W.
Washington, D.C. 20213

Florida Office of Manpower
   Planning
Division of Employment and
   Training
1320 Executive Center Drive
Atkins Building, Room 203
Tallahassee, Florida 32301

Federal Program Information
   Assistance Project
(See G.P.O.)

Federal Reserve Bank of N.Y.
Quarterly Review
33 Liberty Street
New York, New York   10045

General Accounting Office
441 G Street, N.W.
Washington, D.C. 20548

George Washington University
Washington, D.C. 20548

Good Government
National Civil Service League
5530 Wisconsin Avenue, N.W.
Washington, D.C. 20015

Government Printing Office
710 N. Capital Street, N.W.
Washington, D.C. 20402

Harvard University Press
79 Garden Street
Cambridge, Massachusetts 02138

Heath-Lexington Books
(See Lexington Books)

Industrial and Labor Relations
  Review
Cornell University
Ithaca, New York 14853

Industrial Research Unit
The Wharton School
University of Pennsylvania
Vance Hall/CS
3733 Spruce Street
Philadelphia, Pennsylvania 19104

Institute of Labor and
  Industrial Relations
Post Office Box B-1
Ann Arbor, Michigan 48106

International Labor Review
I.L.O. Branch Office
1750 N.Y. Avenue, N.W.
Washington, D.C. 20006

I.R.C.D. Bulletin
Information Retrieval Center on
  the Disabled
Institute for Urban and Minority
  Education
Columbia University
Box 40
New York, New York 10027

JAI Press, Inc.
Division of Johnson Assoc., Inc.
165 West Putnam Avenue
Greenwich, Connecticut 06830

J.A. Reyes Associates
1633 16th Street, N.W.
Washington, D.C. 20009

John Hopkins University Press
Baltimore, Maryland 21218

Journal of Agricultural
  Economics
University of London
School of Rural Economics &
  Related Studies
Agricultural Economics Society
Ashford Kent, England

Journal on Econometrics
c/o Elsevier Sequice S.A.
Box 851
1001 Lausanne 1, Switzerland

Journal of Economic Issues
Department of Economics
Michigan State University
East Lansing, Michigan 48824

Journal of Human Resources
  (JHR)
University of Wisconsin Press
Journals Department
Box 1379
Madison, Wisconsin 53701

Journal of Political Economy
University of Chicago Press
5801 South Ellis Avenue
Chicago, Illinois 60637

Ketron, Inc.
1725 Jefferson Davis Hwy.
Suite 900
Arlington, Virginia 22202

Lexington Books
Division of D.C. Heath and Co.
125 Spring Street
Lexington, Massachusetts 02173

Manpower Administration
(See Employment and Training
  Administration)

Manpower Development Corp.
P.O. Box 1057
Chapel Hill, N.C. 27514

Martinus Nyhoff Publishing
Kluwer Boston, Inc.
190 Old Darby Street
Boston, Massachusetts 02043

Mathematica Policy Research, Inc.
600 Maryland Avenue, S.W.
Washington, D.C. 20024

Michigan State University Press
1405 South Hanison Road
25 Manly Miles Building
East Lansing, Michigan 48823

Monthly Labor Review
(See G.P.O.)

National Academy of Science
Print and Publishing Office
2101 N.W. Constitution Avenue
Washington, D.C. 20418

National Association of State
  Boards of Education
Suite 526
444 N. Capital Street, N.W.
Washington, D.C. 20001

National Commission for
  Manpower Policy
Suite 300, 1522 U Street, N.W.
Washington, D.C. 20005

National Institute of Education
Educational Research Information
  (ERIC)
Washington, D.C. 20208

National Planning Association
1606 New Hampshire Avenue, N.W.
Washington, D.C. 20009

National Research Council
Office of Information
2101 Constitution Avenue
Washington, D.C. 20418

National Rural Center
Suite 1000, 1828 L Street. N.W.
Washington, D.C. 20036

National Technical Information
  Service (NTIS)
U.S. Department of Commerce
5285 Port Royal Road
Springfield, Virginia 22151

Nation's Cities
1620 I Street, N.W.
Washington, D.C. 20006

Nebraska Journal of Economics
University of Nebraska
Lincoln, Nebraska 68588

Northeastern University Press
360 Huntington Avenue
17 Cushing Hall
Northeastern University
Boston, Massachusetts 02115

Ohio University Press
Administration Annex
Athens, Ohio 45701

Olympus Publishing Company
  (formerly Olympus Press)
1670 East 13th Street
Salt Lake City, Utah 84105

Policy Analysis
University of California Press
2223 Fulton Street
Berkeley, California 94720

Public Affairs Committee, Inc.
381 South Park Avenue
New York, New York 10016

Public Finance Quarterly
Sage Publication, Inc.
275 South Beverly Drive
Beverly Hills, California 91212

The Rand Corporation
1700 Main Street
Santa Monica, California 90406

Review of Black Political
  Economics
Transactional Periodicals
  Consortium
Rutgers University
New Brunswick, New Jersey 08903

Reyes Associates
(See J. A. Reyes Associates)

Social Policy
33 West 42nd Street
New York, New York 10036

Southern Economics Journal
University of North Carolina
Chapel Hill, North Carolina 27514

St. Martins Press
175 5th Avenue
New York, New York 10010

Syracuse University Press
1011 East Water Street
Syracuse, New York 13210

University of California at
  Berkeley
Institute of Industrial Relations
405 Hilgard Avenue
Los Angeles, California 90024

University of Pennsylvania Press
3933 Walnut Street
Philadelphia, Pennsylvania 19104

University of South Florida
  Press
4202 Fowler Avenue
Tampa, Florida 33620

Urban Affairs Quarterly (UAQ)
(See Public Finance Quarterly)

U.S. Congress
(See Government Printing Office)

U.S. Department of Labor
Office of Publications
Division of Information Services
  and Correspondence Section
Bureau of Labor Statistics
Washington, D.C. 20212

Vermont Department of
  Employment Security
Green Mountain Drive
Montplier, Vermont 05602

W.E. Upjohn Institute for
  Employment Research
300 South Westridge Avenue
Kalamazoo, Michigan 49007

Westat, Inc.
1650 Research Boulevard
Rockville, Maryland 20850

Author Index

References below are to entry numbers, not page numbers.

Subject Index Categories

The subject index contains the following entry headings:

Subject Index

References below are to entry numbers, not page numbers.

Econometric Analysis

Economic Opportunity Act (EOA)

Economic Stimulus Program of 1977

About the Compilers

FREDERICK A. RAFFA is Associate Professor of Economics at the University of Central Florida, Orlando. He is the co-author of *Damages in Tort Actions* and the co-editor of *Economics: Myth, Method or Madness.*

CLYDE A. HAULMAN is Associate Professor of Economics at the College of William and Mary, Williamsburg, Virginia. His numerous publications include papers in the *Southern Economic Journal* and *The Journal of Consumer Research* as well as the monograph *Land Use Controls in Wetland Areas.*

DJEHANE HOSNI is Assistant Professor of Economics at University of Central Florida, Orlando.